This book provides great insight and a roadmap for creating the energy that is needed to fuel organisations that don't want to fall behind.

— **Steve Vamos,** former Vice President, Microsoft Australia & New Zealand

Michael explores the depth and breadth of any leader's greatest asset—momentum. This book will inspire the new entrant and challenge even the most seasoned leader.

— **Daniel Flynn,** Co-founder & Managing Director, Thankyou

MOMENTUM

First published in 2016 by John Wiley & Sons Australia, Ltd
42 McDougall St, Milton Qld 4064
Office also in Melbourne

Typeset in 9.5/12.5 pt Rajdhani

© Michael McQueen t/a The Nexgen Group Pty Ltd 2016

The moral rights of the author have been asserted

National Library of Australia Cataloguing-in-Publication data:

Creator:	McQueen, Michael, author.
Title:	Momentum: how to build it, keep it or get it back/Michael McQueen.
ISBN:	9780730331933 (pbk.)
	9780730331940 (ebook)
Notes:	Includes index.
Subjects:	Success.
	Success in business.
	Leadership.
Dewey Number:	650.1

Cover and internal design: Jennifer El-Chah, Loved.Locked.Loaded.
Cover image: © pogonici/Shutterstock
Author Image: © Toby Zerna

'Introducing Momentum' chapter opener image: © canbedone/Shutterstock
'Enemies of Momentum' chapter opener image: © Anna Omelchenko/Shutterstock
'Activity' chapter opener image: © jack-sooksan/Shutterstock
'Focus' chapter opener image: © Vladimir Arndt/Shutterstock
'Consistency' chapter opener image: © Rena Schild/Shutterstock

Printed in Singapore by C.O.S. Printers Pte Ltd

10 9 8 7 6 5 4 3 2 1

Disclaimer
The material in this publication is of the nature of general comment only, and does not represent professional advice. It is not intended to provide specific guidance for particular circumstances and it should not be relied on as the basis for any decision to take action or not take action on any matter which it covers. Readers should obtain professional advice where appropriate, before making any such decision. To the maximum extent permitted by law, the author and publisher disclaim all responsibility and liability to any person, arising directly or indirectly from any person taking or not taking action based on the information in this publication.

MOMENTUM

HOW TO BUILD IT, KEEP IT OR GET IT BACK

MICHAEL McQUEEN

WILEY

About the author

Michael McQueen understands what it takes to thrive in a rapidly evolving world.

Widely recognised for having his finger on the pulse of business and culture, he has helped some of the world's best-known brands navigate disruption and maintain relevance.

As a leading specialist in social shifts, change management and future trends, Michael features regularly as a commentator on TV and radio and has written four bestselling books.

Michael is a familiar face on the international conference circuit having shared the stage with the likes of Bill Gates, Whoopi Goldberg and Larry King. He has spoken to hundreds of thousands of people across 5 continents since 2004 and is known for his high-impact, research-rich and entertaining conference presentations.

In 2015, Michael was named Australia's Keynote Speaker of the Year and was inducted into the Professional Speakers Halls of Fame.

Michael and his family live in Sydney, Australia.

www.michaelmcqueen.net

Acknowledgements

Quite fittingly, the writing of this book had an air of effortlessness about it. Despite the fact that so little serious research has been done into the topic, the process of identifying the principles for building and re-building momentum was much less taxing than I imagined it would be.

I have always loved the challenge of making the complex both simple and accessible – and this book was certainly such an exercise. This is not a lofty academic text but rather an attempt to distill what many of my clients have found to be true but have struggled to quantify and put into words.

Despite the fact that writing this book was somewhat effortless, it was by no means an easy feat. I couldn't have written it without the support of my amazing wife Hailey who tolerated the long hours of research and writing while we juggled the delights and demands of a newborn baby. Thanks too to my amazing parents and parents-in-law from whom Hailey and I have inherited a rich legacy of intergenerational momentum.

Thanks to the Lucy, Chris and the team at Wiley Australia. I'm so grateful for your encouragement, support and willingness to take some creative risks with this project. Thanks also the crew at Ode Management who consistently sharpen and spur me on. It is an honour to work with such a phenomenal team of world-changers.

Finally, thanks to the many thousands of clients and audience members whose stories and experiences have informed both my thinking and the content of this book. I am ever in your debt.

CONTENTS

01 02

03

GOING WITH THE FLOW

In late 2015 my wife and I were on a holiday with our six-week-old son when we crossed paths in a small country town with a fascinating guy named Craig Holmwood. Wearing a faded leather hat, dirty, torn clothes, and sporting a well-worn leather whip tucked into his belt, Craig certainly stood out. In fact, he looked like someone who would've been more comfortable in the late eighteenth century than the early twenty-first.

Despite his unusual appearance, it was Craig's profession that I found most fascinating. As we got chatting, he shared that he is one of Australia's last remaining true bullock drivers (or 'bullwhackers', as they are sometimes known) – a profession that today ranks as one of the world's rarest trades.

However, this was not always the case. In the days before machinery or trucks, bullock teams were the key mode of transportation for goods the world over. In Australia's early colonial years, bullocks were among the most important animals on the land. They hauled wool, passengers and timber for many kilometres, opening up vast tracts of new countryside and fuelling the growth of the fledgling country's economy. But today they are little more than relics of a bygone era – sideshows for tourists like my wife, son and me.

Craig told us that, pound for pound, bullocks are the strongest animals alive; teams of them are capable of hauling 35 tonnes through rough and rocky terrain.

'But with loads that heavy, getting off go is always the hardest part,' Craig explained, describing the immense effort it takes to make the first step, each bullock needing to pull at exactly the right time and in the right order – how it's a team effort through and through. The first few paces are tough, with the bullocks straining forward under the weight.

'But just when it looks like they're not up to the task,' Craig said, a smile spreading across his face, 'something magical happens. They lift their heads and relax into a steady pace. It's a beautiful moment when momentum takes over.'

Craig didn't appear to be a scientifically minded soul. But his description of getting a bullock team moving was as good as any explanation I've ever heard of Newton's First Law of Motion. Also known as the Law of Inertia, this scientific maxim I first learned in high school roughly states that objects at rest tend to stay at rest and objects in motion tend to stay in motion. Put more simply: once you're moving, it's easy to keep moving. But if you're stopped still, getting started requires much more effort.

This principle is as true for bullocks as it is for Boeing jets, basketball players and business leaders. The reality is that everything we see around us is governed by and subject to the natural laws of science. Sure, we can ignore them or try to fight against them, but in the end we will find life a whole lot harder than it needs to be. Like constantly swimming against the tide or going against the grain.

> ## Objects at rest tend to stay at rest and objects in motion tend to stay in motion.

On the other hand, if we recognise and leverage the natural rhythms of life, things become a whole lot easier – even effortless.

The bulk of my research in recent years has centred on understanding the patterns, cycles and dynamics at play in organisational life – especially those behind the rise and fall of businesses and institutions.

Back in 2011 I embarked on a research project tracking 500 of the world's biggest brands in an attempt to answer this question: What is the difference between the enduring and the endangered?

Sadly, examples of endangered brands abound. Recent years have seen scores of iconic businesses and organisations fall from greatness in spectacular fashion. So endemic is this pattern that McKinsey & Company consultant Patrick Viguerie invented a term for measuring it called the 'Topple rate'. This metric gauges the rate at which firms lose their leadership positions, and one thing is for certain – it is speeding up. According to Professor Richard Foster of Yale University, the average lifespan of a major listed company has shrunk from 67 years in the 1920s to just 15 years today.[1]

Obviously there is massive value in understanding the dynamics that cause organisations and institutions to fall prey to the natural laws of decline and entropy – after all, a wise person learns from their own mistakes; a much wiser person learns from someone else's. However, I believe the far more interesting story is that of the brands and institutions that have learned to master and even harness the very laws that could otherwise have taken them out of the game. For every organisation or brand that has fallen on hard times, you will find another business offering similar products or services, to similar markets, that is flourishing. Compare, for example, the fortunes of Kodak with Fuji, Meccano with Lego, Saab with Hyundai, Pan Am with Delta Airlines and Atari with Nintendo.

Interestingly, the dynamics of long-term success at play in organisations and institutions are much the same at an individual level too.

If you're like me, I bet you've wondered why it is that some people seem to live a charmed existence. You know the ones. Perhaps they are a sibling, a competitor or even a close friend. They seem to have the Midas touch, never putting a foot wrong.

While it is tempting to assume that uncommonly successful individuals are perhaps smarter, luckier or harder working than the rest of us, that is rarely the case. Nor is it because they knew the right people, had a better strategy, or read *The Secret* all those years ago and constructed a magnificent dream board.

"

A wise person learns from their own mistakes; a much wiser person learns from someone else's.

Rather, the common denominator among all uncommonly successful people comes down to one thing: just like enduring organisations, these individuals have figured out how to master the art of momentum. They have knowingly or unknowingly learned how to harness the natural rhythms of life and get them working on their side.

What can we learn from these success stories? What is their secret to maintaining growth, vitality and momentum over the long haul?

That is the focus of this book.

In part 01, we will look at the very nature of momentum — how you know when you've got it and why it makes all the difference to lasting success for any organisation or individual. In part 02, we will look at five enemies of momentum — common traps and pitfalls that can cause any organisation or individual to lose vitality without realising it until it's almost too late. In part 03, we will explore the art and science of momentum, unpacking an equation for building, keeping or getting momentum back.

By the end of our time together, my goal is that you too will have a clear sense of what it takes to build unstoppable momentum in every area of life. There may not be a shortcut or silver bullet, but there is a surefire formula — and it works.

01

INTRODUCING
MOMENTUM

Momentum is a funny thing. While the physical phenomenon may be simple to scientifically measure, in everyday life it is often relegated to little more than a subjective and fleeting sensation. Much like the wind, momentum can't be seen – but you can certainly feel its presence.

> **"**
> **Much like the wind, momentum can't be seen – but you can certainly feel its presence.**

Leaders will describe the sense of momentum they feel when their organisation is kicking goals month on month. Runners describe the flow-state of momentum at the halfway mark of a marathon when their body begins to run the race with a rhythm of its own. And we all know that thrill of work days when it feels like the tailwind of momentum is our best friend and everything we set out to do happens with ease and effortlessness.

However, while momentum feels great, it can also seem as elusive as the fickle flashes of inspiration – here one minute and gone the next. Although it can be hard to pin down where momentum comes from, we certainly know how to describe the sensation when it hits us.

Here are just a few of the sentiments I routinely hear from clients as they describe the feeling of having momentum:

- 'I feel like I'm in a groove or in my element – just holding on for the ride!'
- 'Everything and everyone seems to be in sync. Such a great feeling of harmony and synergy.'
- 'I was on a roll and everything just seemed to come together at exactly the right time.'
- 'I felt as if I was in a sweet spot where it wasn't even hard work anymore.'
- 'The business is firing on all cylinders and I can hardly keep up with the pace – it's an exciting time to be at the helm.'
- 'We were riding high and felt almost invincible or unstoppable. The growth was exponential and when people asked what the secret was, I honestly didn't know.'
- 'After a while it was like I was going with the flow – no longer trying so hard but getting better results than ever!'

Now, while momentum certainly feels great and can lead to some incredible results, here are three tangible reasons to pursue and preserve it at any cost.

REASON
01

Momentum is generative

Put simply, the more momentum you have, the more you get. In the same way that success breeds success, the energy of momentum always feeds on itself. While it may be slow at first, in no time momentum grows exponentially till you reach a critical mass.

In his excellent book *The Compound Effect*, legendary business thinker Darren Hardy likens the process of building momentum to that of picking up speed on a merry-go-round when we were children:

The first step was always the hardest – getting it to move from a standstill. You had to push and pull, grimace and groan, throw your entire body into the effort... finally you were able to get up a little bit of speed and run alongside it... you had to keep running faster and faster, pulling it behind you as you ran with all your might. Finally, success! Once the merry-go-round was spinning at a good clip, momentum took over, making it easy to keep it going.[2]

The key is this. Get moving – regardless of how hard it can be at first. Gain traction and get the tailwind of momentum working for you early on, then all you need to do is set your sails and go with the flow.

Perhaps the generative power of momentum is most clearly seen in the sporting arena. More often than not, the team that scores the first goal starts a chain reaction. As they get into a groove, confidence builds and the next goal becomes almost inevitable, then the next, then the next. Conversely, the winning team's opponents can easily fall prey to the negative effects of momentum – the further they fall behind, the harder it is to turn things around and fight back. The reality is that momentum is equally potent when it is working against you (something we will explore in the pages ahead).

We all know that if you want something done, give it to a busy person. Why? Because the gravity of inertia has a tremendous pull that can be hard to break. Busy people are already in motion, so getting things done is no big deal.

Remember, energy is built from energy – speeding up that which is already moving is far easier than getting an inert object (or person, or organisation) off go.

#5

REASON
02

Momentum is attractive

Everyone wants to be on a bus that's going somewhere. There are few things more appealing than being part of an organisation, a movement or even a personal relationship that is on an upward trajectory.

Momentum truly gives you an unfair advantage when it's working on your side.

By the same token, the first hint of stalling or waning can cause even the most steadfast and loyal devotees to start considering their options.

Better still, like attracts like. Happening places attract happening people. Inspiring places attract inspired people. Even great opportunities seem to be attracted to places of great opportunity. Momentum truly gives you an unfair advantage when it's working on your side.

I was reminded of this recently when lining up for breakfast at a happening café in the rural outskirts of Sydney one Sunday morning. When my wife and I arrived, having driven 40 minutes to get there, the line was out the door and a staff member at the head of the queue informed us that there'd be a 50-minute wait to be seated. We'd heard from a few friends how good this café's food was, so we decided to stick it out. When we finally sat down to breakfast almost an hour later, the queue was twice as long as when we'd arrived. While the breakfast was good, in reality there would have been five cafés within a five-minute drive of it that would have been as good – and likely had no wait for a table. But regardless, we, plus hundreds of others, fell for the hype and lined up anyway because this café was the hot place to be – it was a business with momentum.

When you've got momentum on your side, you don't need to develop clever strategies for recruiting staff or persuading customers – both will be attracted to you because you are going somewhere and they want to be a part of it.

REASON
03

Momentum is protective

Just as love covers a multitude of sins in the personal realm, momentum covers a multitude of sins in the professional arena.

Having momentum working for you makes you appear more talented and clever than you really are. When momentum is on your side, you get disproportionately more than you deserve through the power of leverage. Conversely, when momentum is working against you, it's easy to appear ill-fated and incompetent – when neither may actually be the case.

Momentum also provides a powerful sense of stability to any organisation or individual. If you think back to when you learned to ride a bicycle as a child, you will recall how you came to realise that speed is your best friend. Naturally, this seemed counterintuitive at first; typically, an unsteady rider will assume that the lowest speed possible is safest. The reality, however, is that a bike is at its most unsafe and unstable when moving slowly; forward momentum is the key to setting off and staying upright.

> **Having momentum working for you makes you appear more talented and clever than you really are.**

When the tide turns

While we all love the sensation of momentum and the benefits it offers, the reality is that we also know how it feels when momentum starts to dissipate or disappear.

The language my clients use is again often the clearest indication that they sense the tailwinds of momentum have abated or even become headwinds of lethargy:

- 'We felt like we had lost our mojo – we were doing all the same things as before but now it felt like we were going through the motions. The spark just wasn't there.'
- 'It was as if things came off the boil. We were no longer the flavour of the month. Our growth plateaued at first and then began to nosedive.'
- 'I noticed the culture internally start to shift. Staff members seemed despondent – as if everything was a bit ho-hum. Passion and enthusiasm gave way to indifference and even boredom.'
- 'Suddenly even the simplest tasks felt like a hard slog – the effortlessness of going with the flow gave way to a daily grind of drudgery. It felt like we were constantly up against it.'
- 'Little things started to get blown way out of proportion. Even the most minor setback was cause for frustration and bitter infighting. It's like we took our eyes off the ball and turned on each other.'

CASE STUDY

Tough times @ Twitter

{

A few short years ago, Twitter was the undisputed runner-up to Facebook in the social media world. More recently, however, a host of new, hotter social apps have taken the spotlight.

At the time of writing, apps such as Instagram, Snapchat, Dubsmash, WhatsApp and Pinterest all rank ahead of Twitter in download rankings. Further still, Instagram's monthly active user count of 300 million is roughly equal to that of Twitter and industry insider Tero Kuittinen suggests that it won't be long before Snapchat is nipping at Twitter's heels too.[3]

Twitter has failed to achieve the mass-market appeal of other social media platforms. One commentator sums it up this way: 'Ask someone, anyone, "Is your mother on Facebook?" And they will likely answer yes. But you ask the same question of Twitter, the answer is almost always no.'[4]

The numbers indicate that it isn't just mothers who are failing to embrace Twitter. Twitter's user growth stalled during mid 2015 and in the fourth quarter even shrank by 2 million monthly active users.[5] While the company's share price had hit a record high of US$74.73 in December 2013, by early 2016 this had plummeted by almost 80 per cent.[6]

There are myriad reasons for Twitter's momentum woes.

According to Kuittinen, one of the main things Twitter lacks is the 'fun, adventurous, funky, experimental' feeling users get on younger social apps such as Snapchat and Dubsmash. Twitter has been slow to make the platform more visual; however, its acquisition of the live-video app Periscope in early 2015 could help.[7]

A second key drag on momentum is that Twitter is just not easy enough to use. Even Twitter co-founder Jack Dorsey was forced to acknowledge this in an October 2015 tweet: 'Our work forward is to make Twitter easy to understand by anyone in the world, and give more utility to the people who love to use it daily.'[8] Dorsey and other Twitter executives have acknowledged that jump-starting growth momentum will require rethinking fundamental parts of the service, such as the 140-character limit.[9]

For Twitter, the stakes are high. They must engage a wider cross-section of new users lest they become, as one technology commentator friend of mine recently described it, the BlackBerry of social media.

Starbucks coming off the boil

In October 2006, the US coffee giant Starbucks was rapidly losing its mojo. The company's shares began a decline that would last more than two years and leave them trading at $8 (down from $40 at their peak). In the face of global economic turmoil, many started to feel that the brand was, as the *Financial Times* put it in 2010, 'a poster child for the frothy excess of a bygone era'.[10] Clearly something needed to be done – and fast.

In January 2008, Starbucks' founder, Howard Schultz, returned as CEO, telling analysts, 'Just as we created this problem, we will fix it.' Re-igniting Starbucks' momentum was not easy, but today the coffee giant is once again riding high and enjoying greater success than ever. In part 03 we will look at just how Howard Schultz achieved such a phenomenal feat.

The reality is that Starbucks' experience is far from uncommon. As we will explore in the pages ahead, scores of other brands and organisations have faced the same predicament Starbucks did in 2006. From Sony to Microsoft, Adidas to Alcoa, and Billabong to Lego, many a brand has lost their mojo at one time or another.

Starting back in 2012, I began surveying hundreds of organisations across multiple industries to explore just how widespread Starbucks' 2006 experience was.

The results have been startling.

A massive 34 per cent of respondents describe themselves as having less momentum now than they did five years ago. These are businesses with sound financials, proven revenue models and solid value propositions. And yet they have struggled to maintain dynamism, vitality and growth over the long haul.

I vividly recall the conversation I had with one particular CEO whose business had faced four straight years of decline. The company in question is a major retail brand that had enjoyed decades of market dominance – until the last four years, that is.

'How do we get our mojo back?' my client asked with more than a hint of desperation. It had been a brutal few years.

While his leadership team and I spent considerable time addressing this question and formulating a strategy for reviving the company's fortunes, an equally important question should have centred on why and how they lost momentum in the first place. After all, without an understanding of what had gone wrong, any remedies we concocted were likely to be short-lived.

And that will be our focus in part 02. We are going to explore five things that commonly drain or derail momentum – what we'll refer to as the 5 Enemies of Momentum. Each of these five in one way or another has contributed to the stumble or demise of almost every iconic business, brand, institution or idea throughout human history.

These same five factors are also vital for any individual looking to avoid losing their edge, personally or professionally.

While the process of losing momentum is often incremental and unconscious, it is also predictable and measurable. If you have a sinking feeling that you may already be on the downward slide, take heart – the game is not over yet. Even if the dynamism and vitality of the past seem like a distant memory, it is never too late to turn things around. In the next section, you will discover that the challenges you face are neither new nor unique.

For those who are still riding high and enjoying massive momentum, the pages ahead are designed to serve as signposts to destinations you may prefer to avoid in the future.

Certainly, I have always found it smarter to place a warning sign at the top of a cliff than to station an ambulance at the bottom! My hope is that this will offer just the warning signs you need to stay clear of danger.

How is your Mojo?

In order to make momentum tangible and measurable, I often lead clients through this diagnostic to determine what their level of momentum currently is.

Read through the following questions and circle the number on the gradient scale depending on which statement most accurately describes you or your organisation at the present moment.

The last few years have been my/our best yet	1 — 2 — 3 — 4 — 5	It's been a tough few years
There is an effortlessness, ease and flow state even when I'm/we're working hard	1 — 2 — 3 — 4 — 5	Doing what's necessary often feels like hard work and an uphill battle
Growth is steady, smooth and seamless	1 — 2 — 3 — 4 — 5	Things are very stop/start — constantly two steps forward, one step back
Everything and everyone just seems to be in sync	1 — 2 — 3 — 4 — 5	Every day tends to feel scattered, rushed and chaotic
Day-to-day operations are very different now from five years ago	1 — 2 — 3 — 4 — 5	Day-to-day operations have changed very little in the past five years
Most of my/our time is spent working on important tasks	1 — 2 — 3 — 4 — 5	Most of my/our time is spent working on urgent tasks

#17

I/we feel stretched by the workload but not stressed by it	1 — 2 — 3 — 4 — 5	I/we feel like there is so much do get done I/we never get to finish anything
There is a high sense of energy and enthusiasm internally	1 — 2 — 3 — 4 — 5	There is a low sense of energy and enthusiasm internally
I/we find change an exciting catalyst for growth	1 — 2 — 3 — 4 — 5	Change is often a source of fear and uncertainty
Our/my efforts feel as if they have meaning, purpose and impact	1 — 2 — 3 — 4 — 5	It often feels like I am/we are going through the motions
I/we spend a lot of time planning for the future	1 — 2 — 3 — 4 — 5	I/we spend a lot of time maintaining the status quo
My/our efforts are leveraged – over time, I/we seem to get more done with less effort	1 — 2 — 3 — 4 — 5	The bigger things get, the harder I/we seem to work
It feels like I am/we are in a groove	1 — 2 — 3 — 4 — 5	It feels like I am/we are in a rut
I am/we are in a sweet spot	1 — 2 — 3 — 4 — 5	I am/we are still finding my/our feet
Setbacks generally feel like minor speed bumps	1 — 2 — 3 — 4 — 5	Setbacks often feel like frustrating roadblocks
Like-minded people are naturally attracted to my/our vision	1 — 2 — 3 — 4 — 5	Getting people on board and keeping them on board is a constant battle
Things feel as if they have a life of their own	1 — 2 — 3 — 4 — 5	If I/we stopped working so hard, there would be would be an immediate noticeable difference

Now tally up your circled ratings. If you scored:

- 17-34: Congratulations, your mojo is red hot. You are already enjoying massive momentum. The pages ahead will be key to ensuring you maintain your edge and keep the energy high.

- 35-51: Well done – things are bubbling along nicely and your mojo is in pretty good shape. That said, there is definitely room to grow and potential to really rev things up.

- 52-68: You've probably sensed for a while that things are not where they could be or should be. Never fear, this book is written for people like you, who want to build or rebuild dynamism and vitality. You are in the right place.

- 69-85: Things are probably looking and feeling a bit tough right now. Your mojo may have all but disappeared, but the fact that you're reading this book means you've got the determination necessary to get it back. The pages ahead may feel like a gruelling boot camp at times, but the results will be well worthwhile.

This diagnostic is also available online at www.MeasureMyMojo.com.

02

ENEMIES OF
MOMENTUM

A few years back, I shared the stage with Apple's co-founder Steve Wozniak, or 'Woz', as he is often called. Woz has a reputation for being understated, endearing and refreshingly candid — and I quickly saw why.

Chatting with him backstage, I was interested to hear Woz's thoughts on Apple's journey over time, but also on where they are heading next. He was particularly excited about Apple Pay and its potential to revolutionise the world of consumer transactions.

However, what struck me most about the conversation that day were Woz's musings on other companies he and Steve Jobs had admired in Apple's early days, such as Atari and Sony — brands that were once beacons of innovation but were now a shadow of their former selves.

While Woz's reflections regarding Atari were no great surprise (the company had filed for bankruptcy just two years earlier and their woes were embarrassingly public), the mention of Sony took me by surprise. After all, I hadn't considered Sony to be a struggling company — until I did some research, that is.

The name 'Sony' was once synonymous with innovation. Back in the 1980s and 1990s, the Japanese electronics powerhouse was responsible for producing wonders such as the Trinitron, the Walkman, the world's first CD player, the 3.5-inch floppy disk, and the first PlayStation and Blu-ray player.

Although outwardly Sony looked the picture of business success in the late 1990s, the storm clouds of trouble were already brewing.

In 1999, Sony's CEO Nobuyuki Idei took to the stage in Las Vegas at the COMDEX trade fair. Two decades on from Sony's Walkman launch, the company was looking to bring personal music devices into the twenty-first century with the release of a product called the Memory Stick Walkman.

You would think that Sony had all the ingredients a company might need to make this new product a hit: creative consumer electronics engineers, slick designers, a computing division, expertise with video games, and a 50 per cent stake in music label BMG. But just as the audience in

Las Vegas were getting their heads around Sony's exciting new release, something unexpected and peculiar occurred: Idei went on to announce the release of a second pen-sized digital audio player device called the VAIO Music Clip, and then yet a third product, called the Network Walkman. Each of these three devices independently showed great promise but, somewhat strangely, actively competed with the others. Sony appeared to be fighting itself.[11]

That fateful November day in Las Vegas was more than a strategic blunder: it was symbolic of the very challenges that would erode Sony's relevance, profitability and momentum in the years to come.

One of the key challenges was that as Sony had grown, the company had become fragmented to the point where their technologies and new products were not compatible with each other. None of the departments was able to agree on a single product approach, communicate with each other to swap ideas, or agree on a joint strategy. Where it had once been at the cutting edge of technology and design, Sony had grown big and complex at the cost of its cohesiveness, agility and responsiveness.

This had devastating consequences. Just a few short years later, Sony had given up on the digital music game and thus paved the way for Apple to storm the market with the 2001 release of its revolutionary iPod.[12] Ironically, the company that had once inspired Jobs and Wozniak in Apple's early days was now scrambling to keep up.

By the mid 2000s, Apple had well and truly taken Sony's mantle of innovation and leadership in the world's music device market. But Sony was also being buffeted by headwinds on other sides too. Sony's profitability was slipping fast and the company was losing its dominant grip on the world's television market, having failed to anticipate the rise of flat-screen TVs.[13]

Although Sony's PlayStation range continued to flourish, it was a rare bright spot in what was quickly becoming a nightmare scenario. Between 2005 and 2012, Sony's share price sank from $38 to $18 a share. In comparison, both Apple's and Samsung's share prices more than doubled over the same time period.[14]

In non-financial terms, too, the mid to late 2000s were devastating for Sony. In 2002, for instance, Sony had been well ahead of Samsung in the *Forbes* list of the world's largest 2000 companies. By 2005, however, these roles had been reversed, with Sony slipping to 123rd, while Samsung jumped to 62nd. By 2012, Samsung had risen to number 12 on the list, but Sony was now 477.[15]

Despite this dramatic tailspin, denial was rampant at Sony in the mid 2000s. Although it was plainly obvious that the Japanese electronics giant was losing its competitive edge, Sony's leadership chose to live in the past, repeatedly pointing to old sales figures and assuming that its current products would automatically reach the same levels its previous successful lines had.[16]

Sony's missteps were not unique through the 2000s, with other Japanese electronics giants Panasonic, Sharp and Fujitsu experiencing much the same fate. Although the Japanese icons were way ahead of the innovation curve in early smartphone design, they gradually became inward-looking and arrogant, to the point where they dismissed the iPhone when it was released in 2007 – believing that their own devices were smart enough. While the rest of the world recognised the iPhone as the game-changing device it was, Japanese manufacturers failed to read the market until it was almost too late. By mid 2012, Panasonic, Sharp, Fujitsu and Sony commanded a miniscule 8 per cent combined share of the smartphone market worldwide.[17]

As Sony entered 2013, things were looking grim. The company had suffered four consecutive years of losses and finished the previous year $6.4 billion in the red. Adding insult to injury, the company's credit rating was dramatically downgraded.

Sony's example ought to give us all pause for thought. Momentum is a powerful force – and once it is lost and working against you, turning things around can be an enormous uphill battle.

In many ways, Sony typifies many of the dynamics we will explore in part 02. Whether you are a large multinational like Sony or an individual hoping to maintain your edge and vitality, in the pages ahead we'll explore five factors not to be ignored.

Momentum is a powerful force – and once it is lost and working against you, turning things around can be an enormous uphill battle.

ENEMY
01

The Intoxication of Success

In the late 1980s senior vice president of the Bank of America, K. Shelly Porges, observed:

The greatest challenge we have as we become successful is not to rest on our laurels, never feel like we've done it. The minute you feel like you've done it, that's the beginning of the end.[18]

The pages of history suggest that Porges is on the money. Success can be a dangerous thing. It tends to erode a healthy appetite for invention and innovation. When you are riding high and enjoying massive success, the lure of contentment and the temptation to bask in your triumph is enormous. Success creates a sense of satisfaction with the status quo and spurs complacency, which dulls our motivation to grow and to keep learning – something I call the Intoxication of Success.

Put simply, the Intoxication of Success is characterised by a mindset that says, 'Look how successful we have been … we must be on the right track.' At best, this mentality results in us becoming closed off to different perspectives and points of view, while at worst it can lead to a deadly blend of arrogance and complacency. Naturally, the greater an individual's or organisation's success and longevity, the greater the likelihood of them becoming blinded by their own triumphs and achievements.

Further still, success tends to solidify people's points of view and in many ways, this is natural. After all, if a set of assumptions and beliefs has led to triumph in the past, information or ideas outside this frame of reference will almost automatically be viewed with suspicion.

Exposing the negatives at Kodak

Reflecting on the demise of photographic giant Kodak, it would appear that the Intoxication of Success played a key role. Notwithstanding external factors such as technological disruption in the form of digital photography, it was also a combination of *internal* forces that contributed to the spectacular downfall of this corporate giant.

Back in the 1960s, Kodak was the Apple or Google of its day; investing in Kodak stock was a sure bet. Former Kodak employee Robert Shanebrook recalls the company's heyday in the 1960s: 'We had this self-imposed opinion of ourselves that we could do anything, that we were undefeatable.'[19]

In almost every arena of life, Kodak enjoyed prominence and influence. Any occasion worth capturing on film, including Queen Elizabeth II's coronation in 1953 and the moon landing in 1969, became known as 'a Kodak moment'. The company's most famous product, Kodachrome, was used to shoot over 80 Oscar-winning films, while Hollywood's Kodak Theatre hosted the Academy Awards each year.[20]

Somewhere between the mid 1960s and late 1980s, however, Kodak went from being an industry pioneer to a prisoner of its success. The very prosperity and profitability of Kodak's film business left the company ill-prepared to face what would become the biggest threat to its survival – the advent of the post-film era. According to former Kodak executive and author of *Surviving Transformation*, Vincent Barabba, Kodak's leadership first became aware of the threat that digital technology posed to its business in the early 1980s.[21] After extensive analysis, however, the company's management concluded that digital photography lacked the quality, compatibility, affordability and appeal necessary to supersede traditional film.[22]

Kodak believed it was bulletproof and used the analysis of digital technology to justify its inaction. When Kodak did finally explore the possibilities of a digital product range, it did so without a great deal of enthusiasm. Engineer Steven Sasson presented Kodak with its first digital camera in the mid 1970s and his superiors dismissed it as 'cute' – all the while instructing Sasson and his fellow engineers not to tell anyone about it.[23] Former Kodak CEO George Fisher explains that the company regarded digital photography as 'the enemy, an evil juggernaut that would kill the chemical-based film and paper business that had fueled Kodak's sales and profits for decades'.[24] Kodak's leadership team even formally vetoed plans for digital camera production proposed by the company's then vice president Don Strickland, saying it would represent the 'cannibalization of film'.[25] One wonders how different things could have been if Kodak's leadership viewed cannibalisation in the way Steve Jobs did when he observed, 'If you're not willing to cannibalize your own business, someone else will do it for you.'

As one business analyst described it, Kodak 'kept its plane on autopilot until it flew into the side of the mountain'.[26] Between 2000 and 2001, Kodak's profits plummeted 95 per cent, from $1.41 billion to $76 million,[27] forcing the company to close dozens of its factories and processing labs.[28] By 2005, Kodak had shed two-thirds of its workforce and the company eventually filed for bankruptcy in January 2012.

In an organisational context, something dangerous happens when everyone starts looking at things from the same perspective or with the same set of assumptions. Groupthink develops and collective blind spots begin to form, resulting in an inability to detect threats or identify new opportunities outside the current frame of view.

Leading Australian demographer and social researcher Hugh Mackay describes how such closed-mindedness develops:

If you've adopted a rigid worldview, you tend to see everything through the filter of your convictions and, not surprisingly, you see what you're looking for. The more you use a particular theory for making sense of things, the more things seem to fit the theory.[29]

It takes great humility and self-awareness for organisations and individuals to remain open to new ideas. Nevertheless, doing so is critical in order to maintain momentum and relevance. After all, before we can change anything else, we must be willing to change our mind.

> **Humility, open-mindedness and a healthy dissatisfaction with the status quo are all vital in maintaining momentum.**

The Greek historian Herodotus identified success-borne arrogance (what he called 'hubris'). Drawing on patterns in history, he described a simple dynamic whereby a successful leader or nation oversteps the boundaries of prudence and decency to commit an act that brings about their ultimate fall. This helps account for the arrogant display of power that sparked the Peloponnesian War and ultimately brought Athens to its knees.

The pattern in human history is clear. The moment we begin to see ourselves as indestructible or invincible, we start making the very mistakes that can lead to our downfall. As King Solomon noted many centuries ago, 'Pride goes before destruction and haughtiness before a fall.'[30]

Reflecting on this, Clayton Christenson in his book *The Innovator's Dilemma* suggests that the decisions that caused the demise of many of the world's greatest companies were, ironically, being made at precisely the time these organisations and their leaders were being heralded as the best in the world.[31]

Here's the key point: the moment you think you've made it, you've passed it. The moment that conceit, complacency or closed-mindedness creep in, watch out. Humility, open-mindedness and a healthy dissatisfaction with the status quo are all vital in maintaining momentum.

To this end, I love Richard Branson's approach to business. The naming of his various companies and products 'Virgin' is a signal that he approaches every new industry he enters assuming he knows nothing:

> *I know nothing, and this will be my strength. I will develop novel solutions. You believe your experience is a strong asset, but it is really your biggest liability – you are stuck in tradition.*[32]

Is it any wonder Branson's Virgin empire goes from strength to strength buoyed by massive momentum?

CASE STUDY {

Seiko beat the Swiss at their own game

Until the early 1970s, the Swiss dominated the timepiece market, producing half the watches sold each year around the globe.[33] Fifteen short years later, everything had changed.

When Japanese company Seiko released its Astron Quartz Movement watch in time for Christmas in 1969, the Swiss incumbents met the news with suspicion.[34] This new electronic watch represented a dramatic departure from traditional mechanical design and was dismissed as a fad.

The reason for such a dismissal was clear. Over the years, Swiss watchmakers had understandably developed a series of set beliefs about how watches were meant to be produced and what customers wanted in a timepiece. They confidently assumed they were the masters at creating quality watches and no-one was going to come in and tell them how to do what they did best.

By the mid 1980s, however, the Swiss watchmakers were in crisis as the Quartz watch's popularity continued to grow exponentially. In the preceding decade and a half, the industry had shed almost 70 per cent of its workforce and two-thirds of Swiss watchmakers went out of business.[35]

The moment you think you've made it, you've passed it.

ENEMY
02

The Tyranny of Tradition

A number of years ago, a team of researchers conducted a fascinating and somewhat callous experiment in an effort to understand the process of conditioned behaviour.

As part of the experiment, scientists placed five monkeys in a room with a staircase in the centre and a bunch of bananas hanging at the top of the staircase. Whenever one of the monkeys would try to climb the steps to reach a banana, the scientists would use a hose to spray the other four monkeys with ice-cold water – much to their irritation.

Very quickly, a dynamic developed where any time a monkey attempted to climb the staircase the other four would hold it back in order to avoid a further drenching. The monkeys learned that climbing the ladder to retrieve the bananas was 'against the rules' and the scientists put away the hose.

After a while, the researchers removed one of the original monkeys and replaced him with a new one. Naturally, this new entrant spotted the bananas immediately and made a beeline for the steps. The remaining four monkeys set upon the new entrant, beat him up, and gave him the clear message that the staircase and bananas were out of bounds – even though the new entrant had no idea why.

Over the next half hour, the scientists replaced the remaining original monkeys one by one until none of the initial group remained in the room. Interestingly, as each new monkey entered the room, it would quickly learn through peer pressure that climbing the stairs was not to be attempted. All of the monkeys would beat the others if they even attempted to scale the stairs in pursuit of the bananas – even though none of them had any experience or knowledge of the cold-water treatment. The staircase became off-limits even though none of the monkeys knew why. It was simply 'the way we do things around here'.

Frank Vermeulen, associate professor of strategy and entrepreneurship at the London Business School, points to the fact that the behaviour of the monkeys is not unlike what happens with human beings. Over time, we too develop processes, routines, habits and traditions that we repeat habitually long after we forget the original reason for their existence.

> ## We ... develop processes, routines, habits and traditions that we repeat habitually long after we forget the original reason for their existence.

This would be fine, of course, if the world around us stood still – but

it doesn't. Things around us are changing faster than ever before and we must run faster and faster just to keep up.[36] Many decades ago, Walmart founder Sam Walton observed: 'You can't just keep doing what works one time, because everything around you is always changing. To succeed, you have to stay out in front of that change.'[37]

And this is the chief problem with traditions. They codify a practice or approach that worked once but may no longer be appropriate or effective. Compounding this, as humans we are creatures of habit who tend to gravitate towards the familiar, the proven and the predictable. We are built to seek out and find patterns. Any certainty is better than uncertainty. As a result, most organisations and many individuals have an instinctive reflex to resist and even *fear* change. Worse yet, we have a dangerous tendency to attach our identity to the past – seeing traditions as central to 'who we are' rather than simply 'something that we do'.

When an organisation or individual gets into this position and change is resisted at all costs in an effort to

preserve the past, a dynamic kicks in that I call the Tyranny of Tradition.

This second enemy of momentum is dangerous because it weighs us down, holds us back, leads us off course and has the potential to sap us of energy and dynamism.

I remember witnessing firsthand the danger of unconscious traditions when working with a major auto insurer a few years back.

The company had been through some rough times. After more than two decades as the dominant provider and brand of choice in their region, recent years had seen a raft of nimble and hungry start-ups enter the market and my client was losing ground rapidly. The company's CEO had engaged me to do some work with their leadership team, looking at external disruptions – everything from the changing competitive landscape to the potential impact of driverless cars.

As my discussions with the company's leaders unfolded, however, it became clear that the key factors behind the company's loss of momentum in recent years were more internal than external.

This was a company with a lot of history and a strong culture – the perfect environment for traditions to take root.

One conversation I had with the head of the company's claims department confirmed my suspicions. I began to explore what the customer experience might be like and whether this was something that needed attention.

'Do you mind if I ask you a few questions about the claims process here?' I enquired.

'Sure,' he replied.

'Well let's start at the beginning of a customer's claim journey,' I said. 'When someone rings your call centre to make a claim, what's the first question your team will ask them?'

'That's pretty easy,' he said. 'We always start by asking customers for their policy number.'

Curious, I pressed a little further. 'Okay. So how many people know their policy number when they call?'

He smiled. 'Very few – in fact, hardly anyone does.'

I could sense I was onto something. 'I'm curious then: why do you ask the question?'

'I don't know, I guess we just always have.' Even as he uttered the words, I could tell the penny had dropped.

Most organisations and many individuals have an instinctive reflex to resist and even *fear* change.

We began to laugh as he explained that when he started at the company 13 years before in the call centre, he was given detailed scripts to use when speaking with customers. In no time, he was running the call centre and so, naturally, he trained new staff in his team using the same scripts he had been given when he joined the company just a few months prior. Presumably, the same process had

been repeated time and time again with subsequent call centre staff and leaders to the point where, now, 13 years later, the company was doing something that made little sense and was very likely having a negative effect on their customers – and therefore the company's success in the market.

Beware the barnacles

Growing up in a seaside town on the east coast of Australia, I used to love walking around the wharves and admiring the boats harboured there. I especially loved visiting the dry dock where boats were hauled out of the water for repairs and maintenance.

I was intrigued to discover how vastly different boats looked above as opposed to below the waterline. Vessels that appeared sleek and polished as they glided through the waves were revealed, below their waterline, to be anything but. Hulls were caked with rough blackish shell-like objects, which I learned were called barnacles. The longer a boat is in water, the more barnacles build up over time, to the point where they can significantly reduce a boat's speed, agility and efficiency. In order to combat this, boats must have their hulls scoured on a regular basis.

In much the same way, it is critical that individuals and organisations routinely and consciously scrape off traditions and rituals that have become encrusted like barnacles.

I remember coming across a UK-based print company a few years ago that decided to take a long, hard look at its internal systems and processes. After going through and itemising all the various elements of their daily operations, they discovered that, from the point when a new customer entered the store to the point when their print job was completed, company staff would write out the customer's name, address and phone number by hand more than 30 times – wasting enormous amounts of time and energy in the process. The inefficiency had grown up gradually, slowly and unconsciously, like the barnacles on a boat's hull.

The reality is that there is a subtle but significant difference between being in a groove and being in a rut. Working with many large corporations and government agencies, I often find organisations are very adept at discovering ever more efficient ways to do ineffective things – and some of these ineffective, outdated and outmoded traditions are the very things sapping their momentum.

In fairness, traditions have their role and place. After all, they can be a key part of building a strong culture, a sense of belonging and a connection with heritage. In organisations, they also provide 'corporate memory', which means that we don't have to reinvent the wheel every six months or panic every time a staff member leaves.[38]

That said, every organisation and individual must make a choice: will you allow the way you've done things in the past to act as an anchor that holds you back, or a rudder that guides you forward?

> **Will you allow the way you've done things in the past to act as an anchor that holds you back, or a rudder that guides you forward?**

While we may naturally be creatures of habit, those who are committed to building and maintaining momentum must resist every urge to get stuck in patterns and routines from the past. After all, what served us well yesterday may prove to be a shackle tomorrow.

CASE STUDY {

Why have three when two will do?

For many years, US military requirements stated that firing a cannon required three men. According to a detailed operations manual, one soldier holds the cannon, one loads ammunition, and the third one literally stands there. The reason for this third person requirement was simple: originally the third man's job was to hold the horse so that it wouldn't be spooked by the sound of the cannon's explosion. Naturally, this role was necessary when the operations manual was written, as cannons were always dragged into battle by a horse.

Despite the fact that horses had been superseded by new technology many decades before, the old three-person rule stuck even though it no longer served any purpose or made any sense. It was not until relatively recently that this outdated procedure was called into question and the operations manual was updated – about 150 years after it should have been![39]

" There is a subtle but significant difference between being in a groove and being in a rut.

ENEMY
03

The Baggage of Bureaucracy

Red tape, overregulation and bureaucracy are the unholy trinity of inefficiency. Few other things have the potential to sap individuals and organisations of momentum faster.

> **The larger an organisation grows and the longer it exists, the more bureaucratic and inefficient it often becomes.**

The great irony, of course, is that bureaucracy was originally designed to achieve the very opposite.

In the late nineteenth century, German political economist Max Weber first devised the bureaucratic theory of management in an effort to combat the nepotism and lack of productivity rife in the family-run businesses of his day. Weber believed that efficient organisations needed to have a 'strict hierarchy or authority, clear rules and regulations, standardised procedures and meticulous record keeping'.[40]

The larger an organisation grows and the longer it exists, the more bureaucratic and inefficient it often becomes. Recalling how this occurred at General Motors, former company board member Ross Perot once joked,

At General Motors, if you see a snake, the first thing you do is go hire a consultant on snakes. Then you get together a committee on snakes, and you discuss it for a couple of years. And the most likely course of action is: nothing.

Reflecting on such an inefficient state of affairs, Perot concluded in 1988 that 'the GM system has to be nuked'.[41]

While Perot's criticism of GM's culture is applicable to many businesses and organisations, at an even broader level there are entire nations whose systems and processes have become so bureaucratic they need to be nuked – or at least ruthlessly pruned.

In his 2012 State of the Union address, President Obama observed that one of the US's greatest challenges to ongoing growth and momentum as a nation is its bloated bureaucracy:

> *We must clear away red tape because there is no question that some of our regulations are outdated, unnecessary or too costly. I've ordered every federal agency to eliminate rules that don't make sense. We got rid of one rule from 40 years ago that could have forced some dairy farmers to spend $10 000 a year proving that they could contain an oil spill – because somewhere along the line milk had been classified as an oil.*[42]

While we like to point the blame at government overregulation or corporate hierarchies for the red tape we get so easily bogged down by, there's every chance that the baggage of bureaucracy weighing us down on a daily basis is entirely of our own individual making.

This is what global business advisory firm Deloitte discovered in late 2014. Researching many thousands of small- to medium-sized businesses, Deloitte found that the majority of individual managers spend up to eight hours per week complying with *self-imposed* red tape – at a cost nationally of $134 billion per annum.

Imagine that. Many of us are being held back by ropes we tied around ourselves.

There's every chance that the baggage of bureaucracy weighing us down on a daily basis is entirely of our own individual making.

To their credit, Deloitte recognised how rife the problem was in their own business and took steps to address it. They now have regular staff surveys where employees are asked questions such as 'What are the dumb things we do?' and 'What's stopping you from doing your job?' I can only imagine the difference if other businesses and individuals took a leaf out of Deloitte's book!

One global giant doing just that is homeware retailer IKEA.

Once each year, IKEA's management spends several weeks working in the company's showrooms and warehouses to ensure that they keep in touch with their workers at the coalface. These 'anti-bureaucrat' weeks, as they are known, are a great opportunity for IKEA's leaders to truly understand any issues that employees might have. As a side benefit, this exercise has also led to a number of key insights and innovations.[43]

CASE STUDY {

Losing the signal at Nokia

The Baggage of Bureaucracy played a key role in Nokia's needless loss of momentum and market leadership in the mobile phone business.

It is a little-known fact that a full seven years before the iPhone's release, Nokia's research team had developed mobile phones with colour touch screens, mapping software and e-commerce functionality. A few years later, Nokia designed a wireless-enabled tablet computer long before the iPad was even imagined. They were a company well ahead of the game.

And yet, according to former Nokia chief designer Frank Nuovo, many cutting edge innovations like these never made it to market due to a dysfunctional corporate culture. Nuovo describes how, in addition to being fragmented by internal rivalries, Nokia's research efforts were disconnected from the company's operations department, which was responsible for bringing devices to market – resulting in missed opportunities that cost the company dearly.[44]

THE 5 DANGERS OF BUREAUCRACY

01

02

Having worked with a wide range of clients in both the private and public sector, I have identified five dangers bureaucracy poses in an organisational context – each of which has the potential to destroy momentum.

Responsibility is shared or shirked

One of the characteristics of a bureaucratic system is that it shifts the emphasis from the individual to the collective. While this makes organisations less vulnerable to 'key person risks', it also leads people to hide behind systems and processes rather than take responsibility for action or inaction. Blame gets spread across the whole organisation. When something goes wrong, it's the system's fault.

Anyone who has contacted a customer service call centre only to be passed from one department to another because the person on the line lacks the know-how, will or authority to solve your problem, knows how infuriating this aspect of bureaucracy can be.

Things fall through the cracks

The second danger of bureaucracy is that, because systems and processes are rigid by nature, anything or anyone that doesn't fit in the boxes on a form or the categories in a database tends to be rejected or falls through the cracks. Large organisations such as government agencies are particularly vulnerable to this.

Just as people can fall through the cracks, so can ideas and opportunities. This was largely the case when Xerox's Palo Alto Research Center (PARC) failed to capitalise commercially on many of its innovations due to gaps in communication between its research and marketing divisions.[45]

03

Things get overlooked

Bureaucracy tends to mask underlying weaknesses and can cause the basics to be overlooked. Take the infamous exploding Ford Pinto.

An engineer strongly recommended that they buffer the Pinto's fuel tanks, but this recommendation disappeared entirely as Pinto reports filtered up Ford's bureaucratic chain. By the time the final specs for the car were approved, no-one was aware of the danger – and almost 30 Pinto drivers died as a result.[46]

This is the problem with bureaucracy: everyone assumes that someone else has 'covered all bases' when it is entirely possible that no-one has!

04

Risk is avoided and innovation blocked

Highly bureaucratic institutions tend to attract certain temperaments – namely those who are seldom tempted to colour outside the lines. Over time, this tendency can result in a culture of conformity, closed-mindedness and risk aversion.

A phenomenon that is common to most bureaucratic organisations is that of the 'clay layer'. This term describes how those in the lower echelons of an organisation often have the best ideas for improvement, yet their ideas typically fail to come to the attention of those who could act on them.

Why? Because a 'clay layer' of middle management stifles such innovation in order to preserve and protect the status quo.

05

Inertia and non-responsiveness

Highly bureaucratic organisations are resistant to outside influences and lack the ability to respond quickly when a shift happens. Nike CEO Mark Parker admitted, 'One of my biggest fears is being a big, slow, constipated, bureaucratic company.'[47]

Bureaucracy is a fantastic servant, but a dreadful master. Sadly, many organisations are being choked to death by the very systems designed to preserve order and efficiency.

In order to maintain momentum, organisations need to engage in ruthless pruning of red tape. This may be unpopular, but it's necessary to achieve long-term agility, responsiveness and momentum.

Bureaucracy is a fantastic servant, but a dreadful master.

Rebuilding momentum at Microsoft

Microsoft reached its peak of coolness with the release of Windows 95 – people lined up for days to purchase it. The software giant's momentum seemed unstoppable – even the Empire State Building was lit in Microsoft's colours. By the end of 1997, Windows 95 ran on 86.3 per cent of PCs in the US (by contrast, Apple's Mac OS only had 4.6 per cent). And yet even as Microsoft seemed untouchable, Warren Buffett sounded the alarm – worrying that the tech giant might fall prey to the very dynamics that had dethroned IBM a decade earlier.[48]

It was a prescient observation. As Josh Linkner puts it, 'Most large organisations exist to protect old ideas, not create new ones.'[49] This was certainly a trap Microsoft fell into as time went on.

The New York Times' Joe Nocera describes how this dynamic unfolded at Microsoft during the 1990s. Once its Windows operating system and Office applications became giant money makers, Microsoft's strategy geared towards protecting its two cash cows. However, once the company began defending rather than building, it became vulnerable to newer, nimbler competitors focused on creating something different, instead of 'milking the old'.[50]

Former Microsoft executive Brad Silverberg describes how dangerously entrenched this paradigm became.

So much energy was expended on repressing good things to play defense and protect the castle. In many cases, Microsoft latched onto technologies like smartphones, touchscreens, smart cars and smart watches long before Apple or Google did. But it repeatedly killed promising projects if they threatened its cash cows.[51]

Former Microsoft executive Steve Stone recounted an experience in 1998 when programmers showed Bill Gates a prototype for a revolutionary software innovation. Gates gave it the thumbs down, saying it didn't 'look like Windows'. According to Stone, this mindset permeated the entire company, causing it to miss numerous emerging technologies.

'Windows was God', Stone says. 'Everything had to work with Windows.'[52]

As Microsoft expanded during the early 2000s, so did its bureaucracy. More managers led to more meetings; more meetings meant more memos; and all this red tape came at the cost of innovation and agility.[53] While Microsoft had once laughed at how bogged down competitors such as IBM had become, over time Microsoft itself became the thing it despised: bureaucratic.[54] In a scathing assessment of how bureaucracy led software giant Microsoft off track in the 2000s, one US commentator put it this way:

What began as a lean machine led by young visionaries of unparalleled talent mutated into something bloated and bureaucracy-laden, with an internal culture that unintentionally rewarded managers who strangled ideas that might threaten the established order of things.[55]

A 2012 *Vanity Fair* article described just how 'toxic and dysfunctional' the Microsoft bureaucracy became as the company grew. It described a management technique of 'stack ranking' where staff were rewarded not only for doing well, but also for ensuring colleagues failed. Endless power plays ensued as a result of this directive – resulting in numerous opportunities, including ebooks and smartphones, being missed almost entirely.[56]

More recent Microsoft initiatives, including the Bing search engine, appear to have also become bogged down in red tape. According to a Microsoft product manager who worked on Bing, an unnecessarily bloated project team resulted in relentless infighting and a loss of design momentum. By the end of 2012, Bing had cost Microsoft in excess of $6 billion.[57]

Microsoft's leaders are taking great steps towards rebooting the software giant's culture. CEO Satya Nadella has made great inroads in stamping out what he described as an 'unhealthy arrogance' about the company's past successes.[58] He has also been willing to cut jobs and favour innovation over existing businesses.[59]

However, the challenge Microsoft faces in rebuilding momentum internally is a formidable one. After all, the baggage of bureaucracy is not something you can shed overnight.

#53

The Fatigue of Monotony

The fourth enemy of momentum is one that we are all susceptible to: simply going through the motions.

Most businesses and individuals start off with an inspiring vision for the future. Over time as things settle into a routine, however, sober realism begins to replace optimism. The inspiring 'big picture' gets crowded out and lethargy, despondency and numbing monotony become the default.

Naturally, there are always going to be days and seasons where we feel a bit dry and uninspired. However, when this becomes the norm, watch out. Purposeless productivity is soul destroying. Emotionless motion is exhausting.

The best way to stay inspired and on track is to have a clear and conceivable vision to be focusing on. Without a focus on where you're going and why it matters, monotonously going through the motions will wear down even the most disciplined and determined individual.

The old proverb tells us that 'Where there is no vision, people will perish'.[60] Importantly, however, the reverse of this adage is also true. Individuals and organisations will naturally flourish when a vision is both clear and compelling.

In addition to focusing on a compelling vision, snapping out of a monotonous rut can be as simple as trying something fresh and having some fun.

This could mean revamping the company logo, overhauling product design and marketing, or renovating/relocating office spaces and facilities.

At an individual level, try moving around the furniture at home, paint a wall, vary your routine at the gym, try a different place for lunch. It doesn't need to take much.

While these ideas can seem like little more than window dressing, never underestimate the power of fresh context.

Purposeless productivity is soul destroying. Emotionless motion is exhausting.

ENEMY
05

The Seduction of Immediacy

I was recently reading about a humanitarian organisation called Outreach to Africa that works with impoverished people in the developing world by helping them plant gardens to improve nutrition and self-sufficiency. The program's founder, Evelyn Komuntale, described how she and her team recognised early on that they could not simply give seeds to the people they were working with, as the recipients would immediately eat them. Instead, Komuntale's team had to explain the value of sowing the seeds so that more food could be reaped in the future.[61]

Although a modern business context may be vastly different from the one Evelyn Komuntale describes, the principles are remarkably similar. In our modern 'seize the day' age where the pressing concerns of the current quarter, financial year or funding cycle can dominate our thoughts, it is critically important that leaders avoid short-term thinking. As James Kouzes and Barry Posner argue in their book *A Leader's Legacy*, 'we must be wary of becoming hostages to the present.'[62]

Reflecting on the challenges facing the Benrus Watch Company when he took on the role of president and chairman in 1967, Victor Kiam noticed an ingrained culture of short-term reactionary thinking rather than a long-term strategic approach. 'We were constantly saying "If we do this now, what's it going to do to our earnings in this quarter?"'[63] Unsurprisingly, the company went bankrupt a few short years later.

While self-interest and short-term thinking often come naturally to human beings, such qualities dangerously impede long-term sustainability and momentum.

Momentum is never an overnight thing. It takes time to build, whether we like it or not. You can try and shortcut it but all you'll do is short-change yourself in the long run. There is simply no substitute for doing the right things in a focused way over time – as much as 10 000 hours, according to Malcolm Gladwell in his book *Outliers.*

In his landmark book *Good to Great*, Jim Collins explores the power of compounded effort using the metaphor of a flywheel. Getting off go can seem almost impossible – after two to three hours of persistent effort, you might get the flywheel to complete merely one turn. However, keep pushing and gradually it begins to increase speed. If you stick at it long enough, you reach a critical point of breakthrough. Suddenly the cumulative effect now means that each turn of the flywheel builds upon work done earlier, compounding your investment of effort. The weight of the flywheel begins to be your friend rather than your foe. Momentum is now working on your behalf, hurling the flywheel forward faster and faster, turn after turn. The incredible thing is that you are actually pushing no harder than the first rotation, but the flywheel goes faster and faster. The huge heavy disc flies forward with almost unstoppable momentum.

Collins poses the rhetorical question:

Now suppose someone came along and asked 'what was the one big push that caused this thing to go so fast'? You wouldn't be able to answer; it's a nonsensical question. Was it the first push? The second? The fifth? The hundredth? No! It was all of them added together in a consistent direction.'[64]

As seductive as the short term may be, building momentum is always a long game – something we'll unpack further in part 03.

My hope is that part 02 has exposed the common traps that have the potential to siphon away energy and destroy dynamism.

However, mastering the art of momentum is as much a game of offence as it is one of defence – it is not enough to merely avoid the enemies of momentum.

To that end, the remainder of this book will outline a proactive game plan for building massive and unstoppable momentum – the sort that can change the game entirely.

03

As discussed in part 01, each of us knows what the sensation of momentum feels like – both when we've got it and when it disappears.

However, while momentum can often seem little more than a vague sensation or sentiment, I would suggest that it is actually something we can strategically cultivate. This, in itself, ought to be incredibly empowering. It means that being in a sweet spot or on

a roll need not be a result of fate, luck or chance. Better still, success and vitality need not be temporary or tenuous – rather, they can be planned for and propagated.

In the scientific world, the equation for momentum is velocity × mass.

While valid and accurate, the reality is that these two terms aren't easily transferrable to everyday life – unless you're measuring the

pace of a Catholic church service, that is!

To that end, I would propose a slightly more accessible formula for quantifying momentum in our lives and organisations. It is a formula that builds on what we know from the world of physics but also incorporates the latest research in behavioural psychology, time management and peak performance.

HERE IS AN EQUATION I HAVE SEEN WORK POWERFULLY FOR MANY OF MY CLIENTS OVER THE YEARS:

$$M =$$

$$(A + F) C$$

Activity   Focus   Consistency

ACTIVITY

I'll never forget the advice my dad gave me when I was seventeen years old and trying to decide what career I should pursue after graduating high school. Having been a school guidance counsellor for years, Dad had seen countless students fall into the trap of 'analysis paralysis' – holding off taking any action until they had explored every possible option. The result: the longer they procrastinated in making a choice, the likelier they were to get bogged down, lose momentum and even their confidence.

'You can't steer a parked car,' my dad said. 'Don't wait for things to be perfect or till you have all the information. Get moving. Set out in a direction, any direction, and you can always adjust course down the track.'

And he was right, of course. You can't steer a parked car. When a car is stationary, you can turn the steering wheel as much as you like but it'll have no effect. However, when a car is in motion, even if it is going slowly or even in the completely wrong direction, you can always steer.

"

You can't steer a parked car.

Perhaps it is unsurprising, then, that the first key ingredient to building and maintaining momentum is activity. After all, momentum is all about movement – being in motion.

That said, not all activity is created equal. In order for activity to build lasting momentum, it must pass the five-way test of being:

01 inspiring

02 intentional

03 innovative

04 integrous

05 intelligent.

TEST
01

Inspiring

Paul J. Meyer said it best: 'If you are not making the progress that you would like to make and are capable of making, it is simply because your goals are not clearly defined.'[65]

Very few of us lack the knowledge of *what* to do or *how* to build success and momentum in our lives – we lack a clear enough sense of *why* to do it. This is especially true if you are a leader looking to foster greater productivity in your team. Stop merely training your people in what to do and how to do their jobs and focus rather on why (beyond the threat of losing their pay cheque of course!).

There is nothing quite as invigorating as understanding why what you do matters.

When dysfunction or stasis sets in, the best way to restore momentum, energy and vigour is to pump in new life by refocusing on the road ahead.

Personally, I have always found that the moment I begin to lose my motivation, it is typically a result of my losing sight of a future vision. Even the most important and meaningful activities can become mundane when we lose sight of their purpose.

I have learned that the best thing to do when I get into a rut and start to lose perspective is to take some time out, sit down with a good coffee and a blank sheet of paper, and start writing out a list of goals or milestones for the coming weeks and months.

I would encourage you to reflect on what it is that helps you to refocus on a vision for the future. Discover those activities that keep you forward-looking, inspired and passionate – rather than merely productive.

#69

THE VALUE OF VISION

01

Most of us have been through the vision-generation process before. Sadly, these exercises are often tokenistic at best and, at worst, a costly waste of time. They look good in the annual report, and sound impressive when espoused at the annual national conference, but often breed cynicism rather than dynamism in an organisation. Even as individuals many of us have been encouraged at some point to construct a personal vision statement.

So, although you may feel like you've heard the vision spiel before, stick with me because if it's done well, vision-casting can be powerful for four reasons:

Vision brings perspective

When a vision is small or non-existent, little things become big things. When an organisation is idle or simply going through the motions, political power trips and petty infighting bubble to the surface with incredible predictability. Just as a rolling stone gathers no moss, a business or organisation that's moving towards an inspiring vision tends to be a place of incredible unity, harmony and vibrancy.

For individuals too, vision has a unique ability to help us see the forest for the trees. When a vision is clear and compelling, obstacles become little more than speed bumps rather than roadblocks.

02

Vision has a viral effect

While task lists can foster *determination*, only vision can lead to *inspiration*. The reason this matters is that determination, while an impressive virtue and a necessary element of achievement, is neither infectious nor contagious the way inspiration, passion and enthusiasm are. That's the power of vision — it lights a fire in the hearts and minds of individuals who then in turn spread it to those around them in a viral fashion. Even the most compelling strategic plans can't do this.

03

Vision maintains a forward orientation

While remembering the past, reflecting on milestones and valuing heritage are important, there is a danger when these things are overvalued or placed on a pedestal. It doesn't take long before the organisation becomes stale, dated and prone to the Tyranny of Tradition we discuss in part 02.

It's a dangerous state of affairs when key leaders or influencers in an organisation are perpetually longing to return to the 'good old days'. After all, while enduring organisations and individuals value where they have been, they are always more loyal to their future vision than their past victories.

04

Vision draws rather than drives

For years, I thought yachts' sails were designed to 'catch' the breeze and allow a tailwind to push the boat along. While this can sometimes be the case, the true design of an effective sail takes an angle where the wind rushes over the sail and draws the boat forward.

Effective visions operate in much the same way. They don't drive us forward as much as they draw us on. The gap between where we are and where we could be creates a healthy dissatisfaction with the status quo that propels us forward — the best antidote to success intoxication and complacency.

Be not afraid of going slowly; be afraid only of standing still.

Chinese proverb

CASE
STUDY

The rise and rise of Samsung {

In 1993, CEO of Samsung Lee Kun-hee had every reason to be happy. Having taken over the company following his father's death six years earlier, his time at the helm had seen Samsung's revenues soar by an astonishing 250 per cent. By any measure he was a successful leader running a successful company.

However, like all visionary leaders, Lee was unwilling to sit back and rest on his laurels – he was more excited about Samsung's future than its past or even its present.

Lee's first glimpse at what this bright possible future could be came on a trip to the US in late 1993. During a visit to an electronics store in California, he was shocked to see Samsung's TVs on the back shelves collecting dust, while the store prominently displayed Sony and Panasonic products. This visit became Lee's moment of truth; he realised that while Samsung was a market leader in producing large numbers of low-quality goods, it offered little in the way of high-quality products. Lee recognised that the electronics buyer was increasingly expecting a sense of luxury and high-quality craftsmanship in their home entertainment. So while Samsung's near-term results were healthy, Lee was determined not to allow his competitors to lead the consumer trend towards high-quality products.

Lee called in hundreds of Samsung's top executives from around the world and conducted a three-day vision-casting session in Germany that would change the face of Samsung forever. Lee's address to the assembled leaders on day one of the gathering became known as the Frankfurt Declaration. It set out a plan for Samsung to be known as a world leader in product quality – a vision that he knew would set the company on a course to market dominance and one that remains to this day. This was evidenced in 2012 when a prerelease inspection of a new smartphone model found that the product's cover texture was off. At the last minute, Samsung workers remade 100 000 covers.

The vision Lee outlined back in 1993 was a key element in Samsung becoming the success story it currently is. As of 2013, Samsung was the largest TV and smartphone maker in the world and boasted revenues topping $250 billion. Perhaps most impressive of all, the company represented a staggering 17 per cent of the entire gross domestic products of its home country, South Korea.[66]

DEVELOPING A CLEAR VISION

Considering the benefits of having a clear and compelling vision, I'd urge you now to take the opportunity to reflect on the following questions and consider what your own bright, possible future could be:

- What would you set out to do if your success was assured?
- What would you want others to be saying about you in three to five years?
- Who is where you would like to be? What is it that you admire about the success they are achieving?

- What would represent a bitter and disappointing failure in five years' time – and what would the opposite look like?
- If you don't do this, what will you miss out on? Foster healthy paranoia and realise that the opportunities you don't seize upon may well be seized by others (including the competition).

DEVELOPING A GAME PLAN

While a vision is the fuel, a game plan is the engine required to convert that fuel into movement and progress. All the dream-board construction and navel-gazing in the world is worth little without an action plan for turning your vision into a reality.

Reflecting on the following questions, what could your game plan for the coming months and years be?

- What do I need to do in the next 24 hours to get traction? There's nothing like a deadline to create some urgency. Make sure your answers to this question are clear and specific.

- What do I need to do in the next seven days?
- Who can help hold me accountable?
- What roadblocks may get in the way of me sticking to this commitment?

In sight but out of reach

Although the exercise of vision-casting and goal-setting is inspiring in and of itself, a vision or game plan cannot be so audacious that it seems implausible or impossible. A long-range vision may be energising, but short-range strategies are necessary if you are to genuinely believe that the future can be different from the past. In short, a truly inspiring vision of the future will always be out of reach, but still within sight.

In a powerful example of the inspirational power of long-term vision coupled with short-term strategy, Dan and Chip Heath in their book *Switch* share the story of a group of students in Howard, South Dakota, who set out to revive their dying community. After decades of declining employment in the farming and industrial sector, Howard's median house price had sunk to $26 500 and the population by the mid 1990s stood at 3000 and was falling.

A truly inspiring vision of the future will always be out of reach, but still within sight.

Having read in class about the death of similar regional communities in Iowa, the students started asking, 'What can we do about this?' They dared to envisage a future for their town that saw it thrive and flourish once more – a dream that perhaps only those with the benefit of youthful idealism could have imagined.

Idealistic or not, the students' vision sparked a sense of inspiration that had been absent from the community for years. Importantly, however, the students' long-range vision was underpinned by a list of short-term deliberate activities. These included everything from a community-wide roster for clean-up days to a simple economic calculation that showed that if residents spent just 10 per cent more of their disposable income in the town, the local economy would grow by $7 million in one year.

Because the plan for turning around Howard's fortunes appeared achievable, the support it garnered was huge. Twelve months later, the local economy had grown by $15.6 million, providing revenue to address other local issues. Within a few years, Howard began to attract new and innovative businesses and before long was a flourishing, vibrant and momentum-driven community once more.[67]

This example of Howard's resurrection underscores a vital component of vision-casting: naivety. There is something to be said for the childlike faith of those who believe something audacious is even possible – simply because they haven't been told it can't be done yet!

Vision that changes culture

By the end of the 1980s, Whirlpool had become the world's largest manufacturer and marketer of household appliances. Six years later, however, it was quite a different story. As sales began to level off and Whirlpool rapidly lost ground to its competitors, the company's leadership decided to embark on an exercise in cultural transformation by casting a new five-word internal vision: 'Innovation comes from everyone, everywhere.'

This dramatically shifted the way employees viewed their roles and responsibilities. Creativity and innovation was now everybody's job. Within a few years, Whirlpool had transformed itself from a traditional manufacturer to a customer-focused enterprise producing some of the most innovative products in the industry.[68]

Let's be honest: a compelling and inspiring vision can sometimes be intimidating to those who would prefer things stayed the same forever. The world of physics tells us that motion always causes friction. When you paint a picture of what is possible, there will always be someone ready to tell you what can't be done. And even at an individual level, it is often the voice in our head that can discount the vision most loudly.

Don't be afraid of the friction. Anticipate it and even celebrate it – if you weren't taking the steps required to go somewhere worthwhile, you wouldn't be experiencing any pushback at all. Remember, stationary objects face no headwinds.

CASE {
STUDY {

Apollo Tyres picks up speed

In 2005, India's Apollo Tyres was a relatively small tyre manufacturer turning over $300 million a year in revenue. However, managing director Neeraj Kanwar realised that the company's culture had become small-minded, resulting in leaders '...constantly fighting fires and spending all our energy on things that probably weren't the best use of our time'.

During an offsite meeting with the company's leadership, Kanwar challenged the group to chart out a path that would lead the company to its full potential. The meeting concluded with a clearly articulated vision: an audacious goal to grow almost seven-fold to $2 billion of revenue, placing Apollo as one of the world's top 15 tyre companies. This vision inspired the team, saw a shift in focus from maintenance to growth, and renewed a commitment to empowering employees with the skills required to win. In short, the vision-casting exercise re-ignited energy and drive like nothing else could have.[69]

Without a doubt, culture change like that seen at Apollo Tyres would never have occurred without a clear and compelling vision to set it in motion.

TEST
02

Intentional

In order to drive momentum, the second thing activity needs to be is intentional. There is enormous power in being deliberate and strategic about our daily activities rather than simply operating on autopilot.

Without a sense of intentionality, it is all too easy to spend our days reacting to whatever is most urgent or recent. Our inbox becomes a proxy to-do list and we race from one externally generated crisis to another. Alternatively, we get bogged down doing procedural and administrative tasks only to find we close out our day never having gotten around to doing the important things we promised we'd get to today (just as we promised ourselves each day for the last week).

Sound familiar? While many of us go into the day with some sense of what we hope to get accomplished, building unstoppable momentum is less about the *substance* of our to-do list and more about the *sequence* in which we move through it. To that end, here is a powerful system for achieving massive productivity without necessarily working harder – something I call the Productivity Blueprint. Here's how it works.

First of all, think of your day as a series of blocks of time. It may be a three-hour block in the morning before lunch, a one-hour block in the

afternoon between client meetings or even the 45 minutes you have between takeoff and landing on a flight.

Now list all the things you'd like to accomplish in that block of time. Obviously, the larger the block, the longer the list can be.

The third step is to consider the items on that list as being one of three types of activities: simple, complex or routine.

Try approaching your tasks in this sequence and in these proportions, as shown.

Block of time		
Simple	Complex	Routine

#83

STEP 01
The simple tasks

If you've ever started a campfire from scratch, you know that it is futile to strike a match and hold it to a log of wood in the hope that it will catch alight. Rather, you always start with kindling: newspaper or small twigs. Only once those are burning nicely and beginning to generate heat can you add more substantial and longer-burning pieces of timber.

Much the same principle applies in our daily activities. Forget starting any block of productive time by attempting the most audacious, time-consuming and challenging thing on your list. Instead, start with the twigs — the quick, small tasks or activities that you can knock on

the head quickly. As you begin to feel the sense of accomplishment, momentum kicks in.

In addition to choosing activities that are quickly and easily achievable, it's a good idea to select ones that are somewhat enjoyable too. You may also want to kick off with a few 'almost done' tasks — activities you may have got 90 per cent completed the previous day that you can knock over in a matter of minutes.

This same logic is behind Dave Ramsey's famous 'Debt Snowball' method. The method says that, in order to be debt free, you must pay off the debt with the smallest amount first. Then you move to the

second-smallest, the third-smallest, and so on.

Mathematically, this may seem counterintuitive — after all, shouldn't you start with the debt that has the highest interest payment? Not according to Ramsey. He says that paying off the smaller debts first builds momentum by giving you quick wins that motivate you to keep going.[70] Success begins to breed success.

The key message is this: simple tasks are more about movement than productivity per se. The key is that these action items get the ball rolling and combat our propensity for procrastination.

STEP 02
The complex tasks

Once you've got a few wins under your belt, now is the time to turn your attention to the more complex and taxing activities before you. Again, don't attempt these from a standing start or you're likely to get discouraged and give up. But once you're in motion, you're far more likely to take the potential speed bumps of complex tasks in your stride.

Perhaps your complex task is the report you've been putting off or the arduous assignment that is getting bigger the longer you procrastinate. Maybe it's the difficult conversation with a team member you've been avoiding or the sales cold calls you'd rather not have to make.

Regardless of what your complex tasks are, a good tip to bear in mind is not to spend too much time getting to them. Sure, you want to build momentum with the simple things, but you want to still be fresh as you approach the hard stuff.

This is for the simple reason that research shows we have less willpower as time goes on. Self-control and willpower are a finite resource that, once expended, lead to reduced self-control and task performance.[71] As a rule of thumb, try and get started on complex tasks no later than 20 per cent into your block of productive time and certainly well before the midway point.

> **Once you're in motion, you're far more likely to take the potential speed bumps of complex tasks in your stride.**

STEP 03
The routine tasks

Now that you've ticked off or at least made significant headway on your complex task(s), use the remaining portion in your productive block of time to get through the routine business-as-usual action items. This may be responding to email, completing paperwork, tidying your workspace or following up with clients.

Without an intentional plan like this, too often I see clients fall into the trap of starting with the routine stuff, then working on a couple of simple tasks and then consistently running out of time to get to the higher-order complex activities – a classic case of the urgent becoming the enemy of the important, as shown here.

As a result, the strategically important tasks that have the greatest potential to cause breakthrough momentum get bumped from today's to-do list to tomorrow's, and then on and on for weeks, if not months. You feel as if you're spinning your wheels, working harder than ever, but never getting the traction you're looking for.

In contrast, by adopting an intentional approach to your daily activities, you not only take back control of your schedule but you will also be far, far more effective.

Block of time

Routine	Simple	Complex

"

The secret to getting ahead is getting started.

Mark Twain

The ultimate KPI

In order to gauge their effectiveness, many organisations keep a close eye on Key Performance Indicators (KPIs) such as profit margins, sales figures, growth rates or market share. While these can certainly be valuable measures of success and momentum, the danger is that they are all lagging indicators – they all measure the effectiveness of what you did weeks, months or years ago.

For those looking to build or maintain future momentum, a far more powerful KPI is one that measures the trajectory of your current daily activity called the Amplification Test.

Here's how it works.

Think about what you did yesterday:

· How did you spend your time?
· How many calls did you make or meetings did you have?
· What did you achieve in terms of immediate results and also what did you do to create results in the future?
· What about your health – what did you eat? Did you do any exercise? How many hours' sleep did you get? What did you fill your mind with, entertainment-wise?

Now amplify this. Imagine you repeated *everything* you did yesterday every day for the next

365 days and ask yourself this: at the end of that year, would you be more successful, or less? Would you be enjoying more momentum in business and life, or less? Would you be more fit and healthy, or less?

"

Imagine you repeated *everything* you did yesterday every day for the next 365 days

Now amplify it even further. What if you replicated your day yesterday for the next five years, or 15 or 50? Suddenly the scalable impact of your everyday activities comes into sharp focus!

If you're a leader, try being really brave and apply the Amplification Test to your team or organisation. I dare you. What if every single person in your team or organisation replicated your activities yesterday each day for the next year? Would your team or organisation be in better shape or worse? Would you be closer to your goals or further away? Would you be experiencing more momentum than you are today, or less?

This really is where the rubber hits the road. As a leader, you can't expect your team to be doing things you are not doing. As Albert Schweitzer said, 'Example is not the main thing in influencing others. It is the only thing.'

Herein lies the power of intentional rather than unconscious activity – it not only means you get more done in the time you have, it also ensures that your efforts are on a trajectory that will achieve the results you are actually looking for.

TEST
03

Innovative

In order to build momentum, the third thing activity needs to be is fresh and innovative.

There is no point flogging a dead horse, persisting with strategies, approaches and behaviours that are no longer working – regardless of how comfortable and predictable they may be. This is the surest way to end up in a momentum-sapping rut. What's more, we all know the definition of insanity – doing the same things over and over again and expecting a different result. As Albert Einstein observed, 'it is impossible to solve problems in life by adopting the same kind of thinking we had when we created them.'

Let's be honest though, change and innovation are two concepts that engender terror for many.

Innovation means taking risks and exposing yourself to the possibility of failure – something many organisations and individuals lack the stomach for.

I'm always amazed and bewildered when I hear corporate leaders say 'failure is not an option'. While I understand the aspirational sentiment behind this statement, the reality is that innovation-related failure *must* be an option, even a requirement, if you are taking the steps necessary to build lasting momentum. In order to innovate, people must have permission to fail. Otherwise they'll shirk responsibility when things go wrong, hide the evidence or, worse still, never attempt anything daring in the first place.

Spanx founder Sara Blakely grew up with a keen awareness of the power of failure, as her father would often ask, 'What have you failed at this week?' Learning early on that the one thing worse than failing was not to try, Blakely developed the perseverance necessary to build a billion-dollar empire.[72]

History is full of examples of failures that laid the foundations for future success. Consider WD-40: the world-famous cure for all things squeaky. While we all know the product's name, far fewer of us realise that it was a name earned through a series of failed trials – 39 of them, to be precise. It could just as easily have been WD-31 except it took 40 attempts to find the winning formula.[73]

CASE
STUDY

Keeping things
fresh at
Coca-Cola

{

Following a decade-long decline in soft drink consumption, especially among young consumers, the iconic beverage brand Coca-Cola realised in 2010 that even they needed to change their ways in order to get cut-through.[74]

The solution came in the form of a novel marketing campaign known as 'Share a Coke'. First launched in 2011 in Australia following an executive team brainstorming session with the ad agency Ogilvy & Mather, this campaign saw cans and bottles feature customers' names in an attempt to personalise the product. The campaign was a huge success, with Coke consumption rising 7 per cent among young Australians and a subsequent rollout of the marketing initiative across 80 countries, including the US. Resulting from the campaign, Coke's soft drink sales in the US alone rose more than 2 per cent.[75]

While Coca-Cola's campaign could be perceived as gimmicky, it worked simply because it caused the brand to stand out from the competition. The reality is that in any flooded marketplace, if you are not doing innovative things that make you remarkable, you are invisible – a truth Coca-Cola knows well. This importance of being remarkable cannot be overstated. When many competitors are doing largely the same thing in a market, businesses and brands must avoid simply engaging in a battle of the beige and playing a safe game.

Building on their innovation success, Coca-Cola started experimenting with new smaller packaging options as well as fresh ranges of energy and sports beverages, fruit juice and dairy drinks, as well as cheaper water.[76]

> **When many competitors are doing largely the same thing in a market, businesses and brands must avoid simply engaging in a battle of the beige and playing a safe game.**

It's easier to give birth than raise the dead.

Getting the bounce back at Adidas

{

Founded by German athlete and shoemaker Adolf Dassler in 1949, Adidas turned sneakers into mainstream fashion items. Adidas's three-striped shoes were everywhere in the US in the 1970s and the company enjoyed first billing as America's dominant sports shoe brand. Their momentum seemed unstoppable.

However, recent decades have been tough for Adidas. By 2014, Nike, Under Armour and Skechers were outstripping Adidas's sales in North America and the brand had undeniably lost much of its cool in the marketplace, enjoying a mere 7 per cent market share.

In an effort to address the long-term slump, Adidas's leadership recognised the need to innovate and try new approaches. Moving away from a focus on soccer, Adidas's North America president, Mark King, took the surprising step of signing a landmark sponsorship deal with Arizona State University – traditionally a Nike school. Sponsorship deals were also signed with 500 National Football League and Major League Baseball players – up from a few dozen in those sports previously.[77] In late 2015, Adidas signed NBA all-star James Harden and NFL MVP Aaron Rodgers and announced they would be taking over the NHL outfitting rights for two years.[78]

But innovation for Adidas meant more than just sponsorship deals. In August 2015, Adidas partnered with rapper Kanye West, releasing the third version of its popular Yeezy Boost shoe with a focus on the shoes' function rather than form. In the latest version of this bestselling shoe, Adidas has incorporated a proprietary plastic from German chemicals company BASF that provides significantly superior athletic performance. Interestingly, this move to emphasise a shoe's materials and performance in marketing is a return to the tactics of Adidas's glory days.[79]

Early indications are that this strategy is working, with North American sales rising 7 per cent in 2015.[80]

Dig the well before you get thirsty

While most of us know that innovation is critical for lasting success and momentum, the vast majority of organisations and individuals don't change until they are forced to: they wait until a point of crisis and then desperately try to find a quick fix in an effort to catch up. On the contrary, embracing change when you are already out in front is the best way to ensure that you maintain momentum.[81] After all, it is wise to dig a well before you start getting thirsty.

Pepsi is one brand that exemplifies this proactive approach to innovation. In the mid 1990s, Pepsi's leadership took deliberate steps to tweak their brand and improve business processes even when riding high and achieving great success. Pepsi's then chairman Wayne Calloway said:

> Some might argue that we should not tamper with our brands in either image or substance. But we don't agree. We know that in a fast-paced world, today's popular brand could be tomorrow's trivia question.

Pepsi applied this philosophy even while the company's Doritos range was North America's biggest-selling snack food, spending $50 million in 2005 to 'jazz up the brand'.[82] Not happy to rest on its laurels, Pepsi indicated its commitment not just to enjoy success and prominence but also to ensure its success and momentum were enduring.

Pepsi goes a long way to proving the point that even the most powerful brands and successful individuals must continually innovate to maintain momentum and relevance. As best-selling business author Robert Kriegel says:

> Today's innovations are tomorrow's antiquities ... Thinking that you can stay ahead by repeating the past is folly. If you or your products

don't grow, improve and evolve, as in nature – they (and you) will face extinction.[83]

The bottom line is this: the sort of activity that builds momentum requires us to be comfortable with the unconventional, unproven and unpredictable. In an organisational context, this means people must know that colouring outside the lines is welcomed – even expected. Creativity must be valued more highly than compliance, and imagination held in higher esteem than obedience.

That's the key message: innovation is also not just about acting differently but about thinking differently – to have our paradigm shifted. As Dr Wayne Dyer put it, 'When you change the way you look at things, the things you look at change.'

Despite all this talk of creativity and change, it's worth noting that innovation need not always mean doing something new. While some of the best innovations may be fresh, they are not necessarily entirely original.

By looking back at what has worked in the past, often we can learn valuable lessons that don't involve reinventing the wheel. I discovered the value of this when on the board of an industry association a number of years ago. At one particular board meeting, we were brainstorming ideas for reviving momentum in the organisation. Stuck for inspiration, one board member suggested we make a list of 20 things we had done in the past. The list revealed a number of valuable activities that had fallen by the wayside over the years. We set about reviving them and, funnily enough, these activities were among the best initiatives we put in place that year. Simply because these ideas were not *new* didn't prevent them from being innovative or effective.

CASE STUDY {

Changing the menu at Sbarro

After Italian eatery chain Sbarro emerged from its second bankruptcy in 2014, it was clear that something needed to change. The company's leadership realised that, rather than relying on mall traffic, they should return to their roots as a maker of New York–style pizza.

The strategy centred on opening stand-alone neighbourhood pizza shops that featured new menus free of the lasagne, chicken parmigiana and vegetable dishes that had been detracting from Sbarro's pizza heritage.

Also vital to the reinvigoration of Sbarro was an emphasis on high-quality ingredients. For instance, Sbarro's sauces are made from San Marzano tomatoes, each restaurant shreds its whole-milk mozzarella on-site daily, and the company made the decision to add 20 per cent more cheese to their pizzas despite the additional cost.[84]

While the jury is still out as to whether Sbarro's refresh will be sufficient to help the brand get its mojo back, it is certainly a step in the right direction. By reasserting its point of differentiation and going back to its roots, the iconic pizza maker is steadily drawing back many of its past fans and creating a fantastic buzz in the marketplace.

The sort of activity that builds momentum requires us to be comfortable with the unconventional, unproven and unpredictable.

TEST
04

Integrous

This underused word, defined as 'the characteristic of one operating with sound moral principles or virtue', speaks to the fourth core element of momentum-building activity.

Anyone who learned to navigate in the old-school pre-GPS days using a compass and map would know the first, all-important lesson of orienteering: calibration.

Owing to the difference between magnetic and true north, it is critical to place your compass on the map with its heading arrow aligned with true north and rotate the compass housing until it lines up with the magnetic north line before you take a step off go.

Many a navigator has fallen into trouble after presuming the variance between the two norths was so insignificantly small that it wouldn't make much of a difference. An easy mistake to make, but a potentially serious one: the diversion of a few degrees, compounded over many hours or days of trekking, will lead you kilometres off course.

In the same way, all the best momentum-producing activity in the world will do you little good if you are unintentionally heading in the wrong direction – speeding up or working harder won't help and will actually take you further off course and away from your integrous direction.

Before setting about a course of action, ensure that there is alignment between what you are looking to do and your core values. After all, innovation without integrity leads to chaos.

I am going to operate on the assumption that you have a clear sense of your core values – either as an individual or as an organisation.

#103

That said, I'd encourage you to consider the questions below and reflect on what your honest answers would be (as opposed to what the socially correct ones are):

· What are the things that *truly* matter to you?

· What would you want to have a reputation for?

· What are your non-negotiables – commitments you would not compromise on even if they became unpopular or unprofitable in the future?

Once you've compiled a list of words that genuinely reflect what matters to you most, keep it handy as a yardstick for mentally assessing your plans. Values ought to be a guidepost for strategy and a touchstone for decision-making.

A case in point is Gary – a family friend of my wife's parents. Gary is an award-winning home builder known for a ruthless commitment to quality and integrity – two things that are sometimes lacking in the construction industry! Over the years, Gary has often said that he will never sign off on a completed home if it's in a state where he wouldn't feel comfortable going back and having a cup of tea with the owners a year on. If the owners have complaints about the quality of Gary's work in the weeks and months following handover, he doesn't flinch at spending many thousands of dollars to ensure the customer is 100 per cent happy.

While other builders may baulk at the additional cost or dodge responsibility, Gary is integrous and it has repaid him superbly over the years. His reputation is formidable and referrals from overjoyed clients have meant he always has more work than he knows what to do with.

> **"**
>
> **All the best momentum-producing activity in the world will do you little good if you are unintentionally heading in the wrong direction.**

Purpose-driven pharmaceuticals

While profitability is necessary to the survival of any going concern, the key to longevity and momentum is a commitment to more meaningful ideals – to be in it for more than simply the money. Paradoxically, research indicates that companies and organisations that have a non-monetary focus actually earn more than their profit-driven counterparts over time.[85]

Consider pharmaceutical giant Merck. In 1935 the company's founder, George Merck II, articulated a purpose that has guided the company ever since: 'We are workers in industry who are genuinely inspired by the ideals of advancement of medical science and of service to humanity.'[86] What is interesting is this purpose statement makes no mention of profitability or even pharmaceuticals. It should come as no surprise that many decades after this purpose statement was first articulated, Merck continues to flourish.

Former Merck CEO Raymond Gilmartin drew inspiration from the 'greater than profits' purpose espoused by the company's founder when faced with the Vioxx crisis of 2005. Although recalling the drug came at great expense and embarrassment, it was a step Gilmartin was willing to take because failure to do so would have violated the very principles that had made Merck great in the first place.[87]

The experience of Merck proves the old axiom to be true: a principle isn't a principle until it costs you something.

Innovation without integrity leads to chaos.

CASE
STUDY

Lattes with love {

When Starbucks' Howard Schultz returned to the company's helm in 2008, he quickly grew concerned that, although the company's stock price was high and business was good, the coffee giant was losing sight of its culture and values. Schultz felt the company had lost focus on what mattered most: the customer experience.

> **"**
>
> **More than an exercise in altruism, these steps laid the very foundation for the success Starbucks has enjoyed in the ensuing years.**

In an effort to address this, Schultz took the unprecedented step of closing all 7100 Starbucks stores in North America for three hours on the evening of 26 February 2010 to retrain about 135 000 in-store employees. It was a shock to the system and a public admission that the business needed to go back to its core.

Taking it one step further, Schultz asserted that one of the company's core values had always been social responsibility and being 'attentive to the fragile balance between profitability and social conscience'. [88]

To this end, he gathered all Starbucks store managers together in New Orleans for further retraining (at a cost of $7 million) and asked them each to put in five hours of community service helping Hurricane Katrina victims before the training sessions commenced.

Schulz later observed,

> *Following New Orleans, it was the first time in many months that I really felt that we were in alignment: 11 000 people were all facing the same direction, and deeply committed to preserving and enhancing the values of our company.* [89]

More than an exercise in altruism, these steps laid the very foundation for the success Starbucks has enjoyed in the ensuing years. Since Schultz's return, Starbucks has boosted revenues by more than $1.2 billion per year. [90]

TEST
05

Intelligent

The fifth and final characteristic of momentum-building activity relates to whether the course of action you have in mind makes sense, plain and simple.

"

Entering markets where a company lacks skill or expertise is a key factor in as many as 75 per cent of business failures.

History is replete with misguided initiatives that failed the 'sensible test' – an assessment of whether something is the right course of action, at the right time, in the right way.

In his book *Humilitas*, John Dickson describes a tendency in leaders and organisations that he calls 'competency extrapolation'. This is when individuals or entities conclude that because they do one thing well, they will be able to do other unrelated things equally well.

In a commercial context, research indicates that competency extrapolation in the form of entering markets where a company lacks skill or expertise is a key factor

in as many as 75 per cent of business failures.[91]

Consider, for instance, how moving away from core strengths played a role in the fall of Kodak. In January 1988, Kodak took the disastrous step of acquiring Sterling Drugs for $5.1 billion. Failing to recognise that producing chemically treated photo paper is vastly different from the manufacture of hormonal agents or cardiovascular drugs, Kodak took six years to acknowledge that the venture was not a good fit – a mistake that cost them dearly.[92]

One of the world's largest cement makers, Blue Circle, strayed beyond its capabilities and also paid a heavy price. In the late 1980s, Blue Circle made a series of failed attempts to enter new markets ranging from property management and brick production to industrial minerals, gas cookers, bathroom furnishings and even lawn mowers. During its diversification push, Blue Circle lost significant ground against competitors in its core business and Lafarge SA purchased it in 2001.[93]

Of all the examples we could examine, Colgate's dabbling in the microwave meal market is by far one of the strangest and most ill conceived. In 1982, the toothpaste manufacturer embarked on what author Matt Haig called 'one of the most bizarre brand extensions ever'. With packets featuring colourful images of vegetable-laden stir-fries, Colgate's microwave meal range was designed to compete with established brands such as Healthy Choice and Lean Cuisine. As you could imagine, the new range didn't fly off the shelves.[94]

Don't fall into the trap Colgate did. A key test for any course of action must be to take a step back, evaluate it with sober judgement and intelligence, and perhaps get an objective view from someone you trust. It may well save you a lot of heartache and backtracking down the line.

CASE {
STUDY {

Facebook's little red book

In late 2012, just as Facebook was celebrating the milestone of having 1 billion users, a little red book started appearing on the desks of all its employees. The book was full of inspirational quotes and credos including:

- Facebook was not created to be a company, it was built to accomplish a social mission – to make the world more open and connected.
- Greatness and comfort rarely coexist.

- Remember people don't use Facebook because they like us. They use it because they like their friends.[95]

More than simply corporate clichés or platitudes, this book served as a crystallisation of everything that Facebook is. It was the ideal way to ensure that the company's DNA was known and owned by all employees – something that is especially important when an organisation is growing rapidly.

In codifying their essence, Facebook's leadership displayed a wisdom well beyond their years – a wisdom that will hopefully ensure the company's core values and DNA remain top priority, regardless of how successful the brand becomes.

> **"Stationary objects face no headwinds.**

While smart, strategic and scalable activity is vital to building energy and dynamism, it is only the first element in the momentum equation.

The second key is what gives your activities purpose and effect. It is vital to unlocking the power of leverage and getting more done with less effort. That second key? Focus.

FOCUS

Without a doubt, one of the greatest casualties of the information age has been our attention span. A study released in May 2015 showed that the average concentration span of an adult human had dropped from 12 seconds in the year 2000 to just 8 seconds 15 years later. To put this into some context, humans can now boast an attention span one second shorter than that of a goldfish (whose attention spans are 9 seconds long).[96]

Our ability to concentrate on the essential is under relentless assault from what I often refer to as weapons of mass distraction. The constant barrage of email, phone calls, mainstream media and social media has conditioned us to constantly switch tasks and split our attention — as much as divided attention is neurologically possible.

Added to this, we have become addicted to unfocused behaviour. According to MIT neuroscientist Earl Miller, every time we complete even insignificant tasks (such as sending an email, answering a text message or uploading something to Facebook), a tiny amount of our body's reward hormone, dopamine,

is released. Our brains love dopamine so we're encouraged to keep switching to small tasks that give us instant gratification. This creates a dangerous feedback loop where we begin to feel like we are accomplishing a lot but in fact we are spinning our wheels.[97]

In a September 2015 tweet, columnist for *The Wall Street Journal* Jason Gay brilliantly highlighted how normal a constant absorption in technology has become: 'There's a guy in this coffee shop sitting at a table, not on his phone, not on a laptop, just drinking coffee, like a psychopath.'

Perhaps nowhere is the constant barrage of distraction having more of an impact on focus than in the modern office environment. Recent academic studies have found that office workers are interrupted — or self-interrupt — roughly every three minutes. The problem with this is that once we are sidetracked or our attention is broken, it can take some 23 minutes for us to return our focus to the original task.[98]

That said, it isn't just technology wreaking havoc on our attention

spans. It's the co-worker stopping by your desk with a quick question, the endless meetings and memos, the conversation between colleagues within earshot you simply can't help but tune into. The modern open-plan office is custom-built to destroy focus.

Just as it's of no value going 100 kilometres an hour if you're heading in the wrong direction, trying to go 20 kilometres an hour in five different directions is equally futile and exhausting.

While distraction dilutes our effectiveness, focus magnifies it. Consider how an ordinary stream of water becomes a jet when its flow is concentrated, or how the sun's rays burn when shone through the prism of a magnifying glass.

The type of focus that creates momentum for an individual or organisation is always a function of:

01 zooming in

02 saying no

03 pruning back.

Distraction dilutes our effectiveness, focus magnifies it.

STRATEGY
01

Zooming in

Classical music has always impressed me. As someone who can only play piano by ear, I have often looked with befuddlement at the endless pages of clefs, codas and crescendos in long-form scores – amazed that anyone can read them, much less play them. And yet perhaps the most impressive feat of all is that mere mortals actually composed these pieces of complex and beautiful music. To be able to conceive the intricate interplay between instruments and then turn this into one cohesive score is nothing short of miraculous in my view.

One of the greatest composers of all time, Wolfgang Amadeus Mozart, offers an insight into how he and his contemporaries achieved the feats of creative genius they did – and it's all about focus: 'The shortest way to do many things is to do only one thing at a time,' he famously observed.

And that is the power of focus. To zoom in and focus on the one thing – the one instrument, the one chord, the one melodic line – rather than trying to write an entire symphony at once.

Beyond the world of classical composition, the same principle applies. Whether you're running a business or a marathon, staying ruthlessly focused on the small things is what brings results.

In the words of celebrated American author Og Mandino, 'It is those who concentrate on but one thing at a time who advance in this world.'

I remember being struck by the power of focus at a conference once when a speaker brought an audience member up on stage. This particular audience member, let's call him Don, clearly had poor sight – the lenses in his glasses were of the Coke-bottle variety.

The speaker handed Don a newspaper page filled with small print and asked him to read it. With his glasses on, Don had little trouble at all. Next, the speaker asked Don to remove his glasses and attempt to read the newspaper again. Unsurprisingly, Don didn't have a hope. He said the page looked like a blurred mass of black and white – completely illegible.

What the speaker did next was what I'll never forget. He took the newspaper and placed over it a sheet of cardboard with a hole cut out just large enough to fit one letter. He handed the newspaper back to Don. To my amazement, Don had no trouble making out the letter and as he slid the cardboard along the page, he read the tiny print letter by letter with ease – and all without his glasses.

> **"**
> **Our nervous systems are bombarded with roughly 2 million bits of information per second.**

Speaking with my optometrist recently, I asked how this could possibly have been the case. She shared that this technique is actually one that doctors used in the days before modern spectacles. For years, people with poor eyesight wore primitive 'pinhole'-type glasses. These glasses worked by reducing the 'circle of confusion' on the retina, thus allowing the wearer to see more clearly without the benefit of magnification.

In much the same way, we are often confronted with 'circles of confusion' – myriads of options, possibilities and stimuli that can dilute our efforts, distract our attention and decrease our effectiveness. According to Hungarian biologist Mihaly Csikszentmihalyi in his book *Flow*, our nervous systems are bombarded with roughly 2 million bits of information per second, ranging from sounds to smells, tastes and touch sensations. The trouble is that we are only capable of processing about 110 bits of information per second. Added to this, the average brain makes 30 000 decisions per day.[99] No wonder we

feel overwhelmed, scattered and distracted.

In order to counteract this, the solution is to zoom in – to concentrate and develop what Gary Keller in his excellent book *The One Thing* describes as an 'eye for the essential'.

Examining the inherent dangers of distraction, *New York Times* reporter Matt Richtel earned a Pulitzer Prize with a series of articles called 'Driven to Distraction'. In examining the perils of mobile phone use while driving, Richtel found that distracted driving is responsible for 16 per cent of all traffic fatalities and nearly half a million injuries in the US annually. Even idle phone conversation while driving takes a 40 per cent bite out of your focus and, surprisingly, can have the same effect as being drunk.[100]

And it's not just our driving skills that are affected by a diversion of focus and attention. Researchers at Harvard University found that a frequent switching of tasks and attention is closely linked to a lowering of productivity in the workplace. Many of the individuals they studied flipped between one task and another up to 500 times per day – dramatically lowering their productivity and increasing the number of hours required to complete tasks.[101] Similar research indicates that multitaskers make more mistakes and are up to 40 per cent slower than people who focus on just one task at a time.[102]

> ## Multitaskers make more mistakes and are up to 40 per cent slower than people who focus on just one task at a time.

As a case in point, Robins Air Force Base in Georgia was facing a dilemma a few years ago. Fewer than half of planes were being repaired on time, causing massive knock-on effects operationally. Upon investigation, it became apparent that employees were working on too many planes at once and switching between too many tasks on each aircraft. Working with a project-management consultancy, the team at Robins streamlined and simplified their repairs process in order to allow workers to achieve greater focus on the job at hand – with the result that now 97 per cent of aircraft are repaired on time.[103]

In addition to decreasing productivity, multitasking hinders mental acuity in some significant ways. According to the University of London, trying to focus on more than one task at a time has the cognitive impact of reducing your effective IQ – essentially turning you into the mental equivalent of an eight-year-old.[104] It also increases the stress hormone cortisol in our bodies, which is why constantly swapping tasks can leave us feeling mentally exhausted.[105]

Dealing with distraction

One of the top distractions in my daily work is email. Whether it's the audible phone alert or the notification window that pops up in the top right-hand corner of my screen every 20 seconds, with each inbox distraction I lose more than just my train of thought – I lose momentum.

According to a McKinsey Global Institute study, employees spend 28 per cent of their work week checking emails.[106] Amazingly, you don't even need to read an email in your inbox to be distracted by it – studies have found that even just knowing an email is in our inbox waiting to be read can reduce our effective IQ by ten points.[107]

The trouble with email too is that it often achieves very little. One of my colleagues refers to this as ePong – the habit of bouncing emails back and forth, shifting our to-do list to someone else and never getting anything actually produced.

Recognising the distracting influence of email, some businesses have taken steps to limit internal emails – or ban them entirely. Paris-based global IT giant Atos took the dramatic step of phasing out all internal emails, opting rather for staff to use a purpose-built internal social network.[108]

At an individual level, if you find yourself constantly hostage to

your inbox, perhaps an email management tool such as SaneBox is for you. The beauty of SaneBox or similar programs such as Alto, Inky or Mailstrom is they put you back in charge of the frequency and flow of email communication. With SaneBox, for instance, the program learns what emails and contacts are of most relevance to you and quarantines all other communications for you to review at a set time (5 pm each day, for instance). That way, you only see what is timely and necessary throughout the day and you can catch up on everything that was filtered out in just a few minutes at a time of your choosing.

Alternatively, put some clear boundaries around your access to email throughout the day. Many of the most productive people I know have developed a habit of opening their email software for only 20 minutes, four times per day. Between these times, they switch on their 'out of office' notification advising when they'll be checking their email next so people know when to expect a response. If this seems too extreme for you or your role genuinely requires you to be accessible at all times, at least switch off the email notifications that pop up on your screen, as I have done recently – it can make all the difference to your level of focus.

In his book *Deep Work*, Cal Newport shares how *New York Times* best-selling author and professor at the Wharton School of Business Adam Grant removes distractions by simply closing his office door and letting people know he is unavailable: 'It sometimes confuses my colleagues. They say, "You're not out of office, I see you in your office right now!"' But as Newport notes, for Grant it's important to enforce strict isolation until he completes the task at hand. 'To produce at your peak level you need to work for extended periods with full concentration on a single task free from distraction.'[109]

In a similar way, Intel's 14 000-member software and services group recently piloted a program allowing employees to block out several hours a week for 'heads down' work. During these blocks of time, employees aren't expected to respond to emails or attend meetings – and the results have been amazing. Within the first few months of the program, one employee developed a patent-worthy innovation during 'heads down' hours.[110]

Looking beyond the workplace to the sporting arena, even elite athletes known for their capacity for sustained focus and concentration are falling prey to weapons of mass distraction.

Australian swimmer Emily Seebohm conceded her obsession with social media played a clear role in her narrowly missing a gold medal at the London Olympics. As she described it at the time,

> I didn't really get off social media and get into my own mind. All I needed to do was focus on my own race but I obviously need to sign out of Twitter and log out of Facebook a lot sooner than I did.[111]

Psychologist Martin Hagger says Olympic athletes should put down their smartphones and get off Twitter to improve their performances. 'If you're tweeting about the atmosphere, you're not 100 per cent focused on the job at hand,' he said.[112]

Recognising this, the Australian Olympic Committee (AOC) released an official stance regarding social media for its Olympic athletes in December 2012 telling athletes they had the choice to either 'tweet or compete'.[113]

While zooming in and focusing on the task at hand is vitally important to productivity, what you do *between* focused tasks can be just as important.

In his best-selling book *The Third Space*, my friend and colleague Dr Adam Fraser shows how taking a brief moment to pause between tasks can make a huge difference to our mental capacity and productivity. The idea is that before you start on a new task, you take a moment to reflect on what you've just done and then catch your breath. 'This is where we have a moment of stillness to focus, become present and prepare ourselves for the next space,' Fraser says. 'This may only last two seconds as you duck between meetings but no matter how long it lasts, rest is essential.' [114]

Reinforcing the benefit of this, research conducted by the Harvard Business School found that a short period of reflection between tasks can boost productivity by up to 18 per cent.[115]

Tips for zooming in

When you are working on tasks that require or deserve your focused attention, try zooming in by:

- closing your office door (if you have one) and making it clear you are not to be disturbed unless it's a genuine emergency
- switching your mobile phone off; resist your FOMO (Fear of Missing Out) and remember that the world will not stop spinning if you are uncontactable for a period of time
- closing your email software for set periods of time throughout the day or using software such as SaneBox to help you deal with inbox inundation
- having designated 'heads down' time throughout your day/week when you can work without interruption or distraction
- turning off new message notifications for email, text messages, LinkedIn and Facebook
- taking a moment between focused tasks to pause, rest and reflect.

CASE
STUDY

Billabong faces
wipeout
{

Australian surf wear icon Billabong is a stunning example of a company that became distracted and unfocused and paid a big price. In 2008, Billabong was a $5 billion company and its stock traded for $14 per share. Five short years later, Billabong's share price had slumped to just $0.70.[116]

> **... the company made a stunning admission that its Billabong brand was 'essentially worthless' on paper.**

In the 1990s and 2000s, the Billabong brand had grown slowly but surely to become one of the world's most valuable in its sector. But it was during the late 2000s, just as Billabong was enjoying its peak growth, that the very seeds were sown for its ultimate corporate challenge. During 2009 and 2010, the company engaged in a massive spending spree, adding DaKine, Swell, RVCA, Jetty Surf, Rush, Surf Dive 'n' Ski and West 49 to its arsenal. What had started in 1973 as a simple business in a beachside Australian suburb had become a complicated corporation and a confused brand.[117]

By late 2012, the company was being crushed by its debt and was rapidly losing its cachet of cool in the marketplace with sales sliding 13.5 per cent in the first six months of 2013 alone.[118] Later that year, the company made a stunning admission that its Billabong brand was 'essentially worthless' on paper.

Reflecting on the company's woes, then Billabong chairman Ian Pollard admitted that the key challenge for the surf icon was to 'refocus, reinvigorate and rebuild the business'.[119] In a similar vein, the company's chief executive, Neil Fiske, outlined a plan to revamp and simplify the company's product offering. 'We have been trying to do too many things – and none of them particularly well,' he admitted.[120]

As HP co-founder David Packard once observed: 'A great company is more likely to die of indigestion *from too much opportunity* than starvation from too little.'[121]

STRATEGY
02

Saying no

Speaking at the 1997 Macworld Developers Conference at about the time he returned to the helm at Apple, Steve Jobs uttered a sentence that is among his most quoted: 'Focus is not saying yes to the one thing,' he said. 'It means saying no to the hundred other good things in front of you.'

It was more than an aspirational corporate philosophy; Jobs meant what he said. Within two years, he had taken Apple's product range from 350 to ten – a move that preceded one of Apple's greatest periods of growth and momentum.[122]

Others have also recognised the genius of Job's approach to focus over the years. In 2006 when Mark Parker assumed the role of CEO at Nike and sought advice from Jobs, the Apple guru was candid. 'Nike makes some of the best products in the world, but you also make a lot of crap,' he said. 'Just get rid of the crappy stuff and focus on the good stuff.' Although the advice may have been blunter than Parker had anticipated, he conceded later that Jobs was absolutely correct. 'We had to edit,' as Parker described it. [123]

Jobs offered similar advice to Larry Page upon his return to the helm at Google. Jobs warned Page that Google was making products that were adequate, but not great, and that he needed to cull some of them.[124] Page took Steve Jobs' advice to heart – within seven months of his return, Google had killed off 25 projects.[125]

Weapons of mass distraction do not only take the form of social media, email or professional clutter. They also include the raft of worthy projects and initiatives before us at any given moment that have the potential to wreak havoc on our attention spans and ability to focus.

At a personal level, as humans we often overestimate our capacity. The harder we work, the less results we enjoy – something referred to as the Law of Diminishing Returns.

Saying no to the good to make way for the best is not for the faint-hearted. Subtraction is always more difficult than addition. However, the words of nineteenth-century philanthropist and financier Bernard Baruch ring true: 'Always do one less thing than you think you can do.'

As Henry David Thoreau said, 'it's not enough to be busy, so are the ants. The question is, what are we busy about?' Knocking out a hundred tasks, whatever the reason, is a poor substitute for doing even one task that's meaningful.[126]

Make no doubt about it, saying no is hard. It requires a great measure of courage as it will often mean another party feels disappointed, inconvenienced or let down.

It also requires a strong commitment to our vision. After all, it is much easier in the short term to keep our options open by saying yes to anything and anyone.

Finally, saying no requires a measure of self-control. Many of us have a well-developed messiah complex where we unconsciously believe that things will fall apart if we are not involved. Added to this, we must be wary of the fact that it can feel good to be busy – even when this busyness robs us of effectiveness.

What does saying no look like to you? Perhaps it means declining a colleague's request to 'catch up for coffee' because you know this will be two hours out of your day by the time you down tools, go to the café, get back to your desk and pick up where you left off.

Perhaps it means giving your apologies for a nonessential workplace meeting that doesn't have a clear agenda or purpose.

Perhaps it means screening phone calls during peak productive times because you know they'll result in a 30-minute conversation you could just as easily have during a less critical time later in the day.

The reality is that we can't avoid distractions and interruptions, but we must manage them if we are going to achieve momentum. It is often the frequency with which we say no rather than yes that will determine whether or not we build momentum.

Tips for saying no

If you are susceptible to being a people pleaser, you will undoubtedly find saying no difficult. Regardless, it is vital in order to achieve focus. Here are some guiding principles:

- Come back to your vision — if you are clear on where you are going, it's easier to know what will and won't help you get there.
- Make peace with the fact that your choice to say no will affect others and they may be disappointed.
- Readily say no to any meeting or appointment that doesn't have a clear purpose, agenda or finish time.
- Resist the urge to feel indispensable and busy.
- Remember, by setting clear boundaries around how you invest your time others will begin to value your time and input more.

CASE STUDY {

Halting the haemorrhaging at Hitachi

The CEO of engineering and electronics giant Hitachi, Hiroaki Nakanishi, recognised the importance of pruning the old in order to make way for the new. When Nakanishi took the reins of Hitachi in April 2010 the company was in the worst position of its 102-year history, having experienced massive losses for four consecutive years. In response to these challenges, Nakanishi set out to turn things around.

His first step was to dump Hitachi's mobile phone, computer parts and flat-panel TV businesses. This was done to enable the company to focus on its more profitable infrastructure projects such as power plants, rail lines and water treatment facilities. The effects of this pruning exercise were swift and stunning – by the end of 2011, Hitachi was back in the black with a $4.35 billion profit.[127]

Fellow Japanese electronics giant Panasonic recently announced it will no longer tolerate unprofitable units in its sprawling pool of businesses. The company said it will halt losses in unprofitable lines such as semiconductors, mobile phones and its once mighty but now flagging television operations.[128]

"

If you chase two rabbits, you will catch neither one.

Russian proverb

STRATEGY
03

Pruning back

While zooming in and saying no are powerful pre-emptive strategies for safeguarding focus, what do you do when you realise that your plate is already overloaded, your organisation is bloated or you feel bogged down by the commitments you've already made? To answer that question, look no further than the world of horticulture.

The third element of focus is one that avid gardeners would well understand the importance of.

In order for a garden to thrive, planting, watering and even weeding are not enough; at times more drastic steps need to be taken. Branches, foliage and even entire trees need to be cut away for the good of the garden as a whole.

Broadly speaking, pruning serves three purposes:

a. *Vitality.* Dead and diseased branches are potential sources of infection.[129] Old growth also inhibits the penetration of light and air that is necessary in order to encourage new growth.[130]

b. *Strategy.* Pruning helps to stimulate fruit growth by not allowing the tree to focus its energies as it would naturally in the production of roots or foliage.[131]

c. *Symmetry.* Pruning helps to maintain balance in the framework of branches.[132]

CASE
STUDY

Lessons in
longevity from
Lego

{

Perhaps the best example of the power of pruning in restoring momentum to an ailing business would be that of Lego.

The iconic Danish toymaker has certainly had its fair share of troubles as new technologies threatened to take its place in the hearts and minds of children in the 1990s and early 2000s.[133] By the end of 2003, for instance, Lego's sales had plunged by 30 per cent in one year; the company had racked up debt of $800 million[134] and was teetering on the edge of bankruptcy.[135]

Just over a decade later, Lego's recovery had been nothing short of breathtaking. In September 2014, for instance, they overtook Mattel as the world's biggest toymaker – an enormous accomplishment by any measure.[136] Less than a year later, Lego was named the world's most powerful brand and was voted the most popular toy of all time.[137]

What led to such a dramatic turnaround? Certainly innovation played a key role. The company's ventures into video games, digital toy platforms, robotics and even board games have paid enormous dividends.[138] Better still, perhaps the greatest stroke of genius has been Lego's range of play sets designed especially for girls, called Lego Friends. So successful has the female focus been that by the middle of 2012, 27 per cent of all Lego play sets sold in the US were purchased by or for girls.[139]

And yet it was Lego's pruning efforts that perhaps best explain the company's incredible revival.

In a 2001 interview with *Fast Company*, grandson of Lego's founder and the company's then president Kjeld Kirk Kristiansen conceded that, by the mid 1990s, Lego had become a slow company. 'We were a heavy institution. We were losing our dynamism,' he said.[140]

In an effort to address this loss of dynamism, Kristiansen and his fellow executives embarked on a frenetic pursuit of innovation. For a time, the strategy worked. The Lego Group's sales increased 17 per cent from 2000 to 2002. But in the early months of 2003, the Lego empire began to crack. Retailers such as Target and Walmart were choking on a backlog of unsold Lego sets from Christmas 2002. Inventory ballooned by 40 per cent in some outlets.[141]

This dilemma was not due to too little innovation but rather to a shocking lack of *profitable* innovation. All the creativity from the previous few years had generated a wealth of new products, but only 6 per cent were actually making money.[142]

Amidst this new and somewhat deeper crisis, a new Lego CEO by the name of Jorgen Knudstorp was appointed in 2004. Knudstorp quickly identified that the Lego Group had over-innovated, spread itself far too thin and launched so many new initiatives that the company had lost a 'crisp sense of identity'.[143] In short, the company was in desperate need of a prune and Knudstorp was just the man to do it.

A key focus on turnaround strategy was to return to 'core products'. Lego sold off assets such as the LEGOLAND theme parks and eliminated almost 30 per cent of the company's product lines.[144]

Production processes also required attention. In just the seven years from 1997 to 2004 the number of elements in the company's inventory had exploded, ascending from slightly more than 6000 to more than 14 200. So had its range of colours, from the original six to more than 50. Ninety per cent of the new elements were used just once, and with all this increased complexity manufacturing costs skyrocketed.

Knudstorp's strategy was to reduce the number of components in Lego's product portfolio by a full 50 per cent.[145]

The results were almost immediate. By the end of 2005, Lego rebounded from a $292 million loss the previous year to a pre-tax profit of $117 million.[146] That same year, the company would post sales of $1.2 billion but, more importantly, profitability would more than triple.[147]

Today, children around the world spend a combined 5 billion hours playing with Lego's various products each year. Every second, seven Lego sets are sold somewhere on the planet, with Lego's extensive network of factories churning out a staggering 22 billion plastic bricks each year – roughly 500 bricks per second.[148] The reality, though, is that Lego is only enjoying this staggering level of momentum because it was willing to prune.

As evidenced in Lego's example, pruning is vital for any individual and organisation committed to maintaining focus and building momentum. Before you hastily get out your shears, however, remember to prune with the same three ends in mind that a gardener would: vitality, strategy and symmetry.

A. VITALITY

Pruning the past in order to make way for the future is a critically important element of maintaining focus.

As we see in part 02, traditions and bureaucracy are often self-sabotaging – causing an individual or organisation to get held back and bogged down.

Vitality-driven pruning sometimes means dispensing with traditions that no longer serve a purpose. Other times it means being willing to leave behind mental models or paradigms that have become constrictive rather than constructive. It could even be as simple as shedding unnecessary weight – metaphorically or literally.

In the world of aviation, weight means everything to efficiency. For instance, each coat of paint on a commercial jetliner can weigh up to 251 kilograms. Though only 4 millimetres thick, even this single coat of paint can increase fuel consumption considerably and so airlines tend to never allow planes to carry more than two layers of paint. Every third time the plane is refurbished, all the paint must be removed and the surface brought back to the bare metal.[149]

In the same way, individuals and organisations would do well to routinely press the refresh button and shed some of the vestiges of the past before adding anything new.

Vitality-driven pruning sometimes means dispensing with traditions that no longer serve a purpose.

Never confuse
action with activity.

Benjamin Franklin

CASE
STUDY

Sony slims down {

As discussed in part 02, Sony was once the epitome of vitality and agility. In the 1980s and 1990s, the Japanese electronics giant was responsible for producing wonders such as the world's first CD player, the Blu-ray player, the Walkman, the 3.5-inch floppy disk, the PlayStation and the Triniton.[150] Steve Jobs was so inspired by Sony that he used it as his model in Apple's early days.[151]

Like many successful companies, however, Sony got stuck. Where it had once been at the cutting edge of technology and design, the company grew big and complex at the cost of its agility and responsiveness. For years, Sony continued to enter too many new markets for the sake of being in them instead of defining them.[152] They were late to embrace LCD televisions; slow to react to the iPhone; and their answer to Apple's iPad reached the market six months after Apple had released a second edition of its tablet computer.[153] Ironically, the company that had once inspired Apple was now scrambling to keep up.

In April 2012 new Sony CEO Kazuo Hirai identified that the company's number one problem was its lack of speed in responding to marketplace events.[154] To address this, Hirai got out his pruning shears. His first step was to end Sony's decade-long marriage with Swedish mobile phone company Ericsson. Next to go were any Sony-owned non-core companies, including a chemical-products business and a unit that specialised in producing small and midsized LCD displays.[155] Hirai also trimmed Sony's global workforce by roughly 10 000 employees[156] and streamlined manufacturing processes so that Sony's TV business expenses were slashed by half. Even Sony's profitable music-publishing arm looks likely to be sold off, with company leadership suggesting it no longer meshes with Sony's other businesses.[157]

Speaking of his resolve to turn Sony around even in the face of stiff opposition, Kazuo Hirai proclaimed, 'There is no time but now for Sony to change. We can't turn away from making painful decisions.'[158]

At the time of writing, the revitalisation of Sony is gathering pace. The company's net profit in the second quarter of 2015 nearly tripled, reaching $685 million.

B. STRATEGY

Pruning dead wood is pretty easy – after all, dead wood is obvious. It's typically brown, dry and lifeless. However, the skill of a true gardener is to have the courage and discernment to prune what is still living in the long-term best interests of the whole plant.

Although it goes against conventional thinking, sometimes it is actually necessary for organisations to prune products and initiatives that are highly profitable. After all, although these products and initiatives may be successful in the marketplace, they may no longer be a strategic fit with the organisation – therefore they need to go. Recognising this, consumer goods behemoth Procter & Gamble (P&G) announced in

August 2014 that it would cull more than half of its brands in a bold effort to become nimbler and speed up its growth. 'I'm not interested in size at all,' chief executive A. G. Lafley said, 'I'm interested in whether we are the preferred choice of shoppers.'[159]

To see another brilliant example of pruning the good to make way for the best, look at pioneering science company DuPont. For over two centuries, DuPont has been at the cutting edge of bringing scientific discoveries to market. Although the company's origins were in the manufacture of gunpowder and dynamite, in the early 1900s DuPont began focusing on products and technologies that would lead to the betterment of society.

Over the following decades, DuPont was responsible for the invention of numerous landmark products such as nylon, Teflon and lycra. More recently, the company turned its attention to innovation and invention in the areas of food, fuel and people security, each with a strong emphasis on sustainability.

What is impressive about DuPont is not the array of new products it has pioneered, but the long list of old ones it has deliberately left behind. Because the strategic focus of DuPont is to continually bring new science to market, the company has realised the need to divest itself of the very brands and businesses that made it successful in the first place. It is this ruthless commitment to pruning that has allowed DuPont to maintain momentum and vitality when many of its rivals have fallen by the wayside.

For organisations, strategic pruning is vital in addressing inefficiencies that can act as a drag on momentum and a diffusion of focus.

Giving an organisation a quick trim is often the first port of call when leaders are looking to get an entity's mojo back. When Meg Whitman took the reins at HP in September 2011, for instance, she made job cuts her first step to reorganising and reviving the company and she made it clear that no position was beyond scrutiny.[160]

In October 2014 Whitman took this a step further, splitting HP in two. She said the breakup would make the company nimbler and enable it to invest in the products and acquisitions necessary to keep pace with the market.[161]

In one of the boldest pruning initiatives I've come across, one small business owner I crossed paths with a few years back took the step of cancelling his old mobile phone number and getting a brand new one. The reason for this somewhat unconventional move was that his business had enjoyed years of massive growth but, as operations had expanded, he'd given every staff member his mobile phone number in case they needed it. Now spread across multiple offices and states, the volume of calls was relentless and had become a handbrake on growth. Staff rarely took initiative or solved problems themselves because they knew the boss was only a phone call away.

Once this business owner had a new number, he only gave it out to a strategically small group of people within the business. While the change certainly took some adjustment for him and his staff, the results over time were tremendous. Initiative, creativity and productivity grew exponentially in the months and years that followed.

At an individual level, what does strategic pruning look like for you? You may not need to change your mobile phone number, but perhaps it means unsubscribing from email newsletters you never read, deleting apps and games on your phone that distract you, or simply clearing away clutter on your desk.

C. SYMMETRY

The final element of pruning centres on the importance of balance.

If individuals or organisations are too heavily focused on one area at the expense of others, long-term and sustainable growth will be near impossible.

The reality is that life is never in perfect balance. Success and fruitfulness in one area often comes at the expense of another:

- We focus on working hard to provide for our families only to find that we lack the time to enjoy those we love and the things we are providing for them.
- We cut back work hours in order to embrace a simpler life and realise that our career is stalling.
- We get involved in the community in an attempt to give back and realise that we now lack the time to exercise and keep fit.
- We enrol in a course to advance our skills or career and our friends begin complaining we are never around anymore.

It's the same in business or organisational life:

- You decide to focus on sales and new business development only to notice six months down the track that existing customers are showing signs of dissatisfaction and switching to the competition.
- You decide to invest in your staff through training and development only to find that your bottom line now leaves little room for new product research and innovation.
- You successfully break into a new market overseas only to find that your larger home base begins faltering and showing signs of neglect a year on from the expansion.

Achieving symmetry is never a set-and-forget thing for organisations and businesses. Constant vigilance and course corrections are necessary if you are going to stay on track.

Tips for
pruning back

If your plate is full and your organisation is feeling bloated or bogged down, consider pruning back with the following principles in mind:

- Identify outdated traditions and bureaucratic red tape (self-imposed or not) that may be hindering your vitality and agility.

- Be realistic about your capacity and remember the rule of thumb: always do one less thing than you think you can.

- Aim for simplicity and dispense with any clutter that has the potential to slow you down.

- Recognise that while balance is never completely attainable, it is a worthy goal to consistently aim for.

- Be mindful that sometimes it is people who need to be pruned from our lives – especially those who have a destructive, derailing and distracting effect through their attitude or influence.

CASE STUDY {

Rebooting IBM

Although IBM had been one of the great corporate success stories of the twentieth century, the 1980s and then early 1990s saw the company stumble spectacularly.

In 1993, Lou Gerstner took the helm and quickly set about turning around IBM's fortunes. He began by pruning any executives who failed to share his sense of urgency for change, or who fell short of delivering on their responsibilities. Gerstner was a stickler for responsibility and accountability. Gerstner's management team then had to face up to just how bad things had become. The company's mainframe computers were overpriced and quickly losing market share, and a culture of bureaucracy, inefficiency and entitlement had spread throughout the organisation. Following this sobering analysis, Gerstner embarked on a ruthless and incredibly effective pruning agenda that included:

· ceasing production of applications software development
· explicitly linking employee benefits with results and performance
· thoroughly re-engineering almost all company processes, with $14 billion worth of inefficiencies eliminated between 1993 and 2002.[162]

Although IBM has come a long way, recent years have seen the company's leadership revisit many of the principles that guided Gerstner in the 1990s. While IBM is gradually expanding into data analytics, cloud and mobile technology, the problem is that two thirds of its revenue is derived from legacy assets.[163] In April 2013, the newly appointed CEO, Ginni Rometty acknowledged that the sprawling technology company needed to move faster and respond more quickly to customers.[164]

It has been said that the successful person is little more than the average person, focused. I wholeheartedly believe this to be true.

So far in this part we have explored the vital element of activity and the critical role of focus in building momentum. However, the third and final ingredient to building dynamism and vitality that lasts is the great multiplier of both activity and focus: consistency.

CONSISTENCY

For me, one of the true delights of becoming a father was the rediscovery of my favourite childhood books as I read them to my son. From *The Very Hungry Caterpillar* to *The Velveteen Rabbit* and *The Wind in the Willows*, I loved watching his delight as he fell in love with the characters and plots just as I had three decades earlier.

I was reminded too of how many of the stories we read our kids are filled with powerful lessons for life – there is a reason the 'moral of the story' is called just that! From the importance of sharing to the value of honesty, so many of the lessons in kids' books are ones many of us adults would do well to revisit.

And yet, the childhood story that perhaps offers the most poignant lesson for building momentum is the legendary Aesop's fable *The Tortoise and the Hare*. In case you're a little hazy on the details, this little fable tells the story of a slow-moving tortoise who grows tired of the boastful taunts of a hare and challenges him to a race. As would be expected, the race begins and the hare streaks way ahead and, confident of his certain win, takes a nap at the halfway mark.

The tortoise, however, plodding along, crawls slowly past his sleeping opponent and (spoiler alert!) wins the race. The tortoise may not have been the fastest, the sexiest or the most gifted, but the victory was his nonetheless.

Even those who may not remember the details of this fable know the moral to the story: slow and steady wins the race.

As it is in business and life.

Just as many droplets of water make a waterfall, many consistent actions, big and small, over time will build momentum. A trickle at first, but it will eventually become a roaring torrent stronger than anything that can be put in its way.

In honesty, I wish this were not the case. Consistency is a tough sell. It isn't glamorous or fun. Human nature loves an easy win. We gravitate towards the path of least resistance. Our quick-fix culture reflects and reinforces this. Infomercials tempt us with offers that will help us get fitter, richer and younger overnight and with three easy payments of $49.95.

While we love the instant gratification sales pitch and secretly hope it will work this time, we know in our heart of hearts that this isn't the way life works.

Past generations may have been less susceptible to the marketing hype that so easily seduces us today. After all, many of our forebears grew up on or connected to the land and recognised that there is always a lag time between sowing and reaping. They knew that Rome wasn't built in a day and that nothing worthwhile in life is either.

As I write these words, we have just clicked over into a new year and much of the media coverage is on New Year's resolutions — why we make them and why we rarely keep them. Although psychologists offer complex and plausible explanations, the simple reason most of us find consistency and discipline

so difficult is that deep down we're not sure it will be worth the effort. Discipline's vivid and painful short-term price often outweighs the vague and distant rewards on offer. And what's more, we wonder whether anything we do is actually making a difference or whether our efforts are in vain. Imagine how much more rewarding exercise would be if calories screamed as you burned them!

Of all the explanations as to why consistency is so difficult to maintain, I believe the most telling is this: as humans we *overestimate* the impact of our decisions in the short term but grossly *underestimate* their impact in the long term.

In his insightful book *The Slight Edge*, Jeff Olsen powerfully illustrates this through the allegorical tale of

a wealthy father who summoned his two sons to his bedside in his final days. The father produced two polished timber boxes and explained that each son would need to choose which one they would like to receive as their father's parting gift.

The father opened the first box and inside were 1000 crisp, new $1000 notes — one million dollars in cash. Opening the second box, he revealed a single shiny copper penny.

If face value was all that mattered, the decision would be a simple one. But there was a catch. 'If you take the penny, I will instruct my financial manager to ensure that it is doubled each day for the next month.'

After a period of reflection, the first son chose the $1 million and immediately set out to invest the money in the hope of turning his million dollars into even more. The second son, however, opted for the penny on a hunch that there may have been a point his father was looking to make. A few hours later, the father passed away, his two sons at his side.

Before going their separate ways, the boys decided to check in with each other each week to see how they were going with their respective inheritances. One week down the track, the first brother had made a few savvy investments and had already increased his inheritance by a tidy sum. The second brother, however, had only amassed 64 cents – his penny having doubled in value each day for the preceding seven days. In sympathy, the first son urged his brother to go back to their father's financier and say he had changed his mind. 'Even if he only gives you half a million dollars, it's certainly better than scraping by on what you've got now.' But the second son decided to stay the course.

By the next catch-up at day 14, things didn't look very different. The first son's investment portfolio had taken a battering in recent days but his nest egg was still a sizeable sum. The second son's penny stash had grown nicely but still only amounted to $81.92. By the beginning of the third week, it was still only $655.35.

On the fourth week, though, 28 days after receiving their father's inheritance, something interesting occurred. The two brothers sat down as usual but the second son seemed to have a different posture from the week before. While the older brother was still tracking well financially and felt conformable in the decision he'd made almost a month earlier, what he didn't realise was that the second son's inheritance had passed the million-dollar mark just a few hours earlier at the stroke of midnight. And what's more, there were still 3 days to go in the month. By day 29, the second son's fortune increased to over $2.5 million and, by the end of the month it amounted to the phenomenal sum of $10 737 418 – more than ten times the older brother's fortune.[165]

While the story may be allegorical, the principle it expounds is far from it. What financiers refer to as compound interest and mathematicians would describe as a geometric progression I like to call the Law of Cumulative Effect.

Consider the power of the Law of Cumulative Effect

If you fold a large piece of paper once, then twice, then over and over again till the original piece had been folded 50 times (assuming that were possible), how tall would the folded paper stack be? It may surprise you to learn that the stack would be taller than your house or even Dubai's Burj Khalifa. In fact, the stack of paper would be taller than the distance of the earth to the sun and back again.[166]

An experiment conducted by San Francisco's Exploratorium in 2001 discovered that a single domino is capable of knocking down another domino 50 per cent larger in size. While this may not appear to be an earth-shattering discovery, the implications are actually enormous. For instance, if you started with a regular 5-centimetre-high domino, within eight dominoes you could fell one that was 90 centimetres tall; the twenty-third could be as high as the Eiffel Tower; the thirty-first would be taller than Mount Everest; and the fifty-seventh would be taller than the distance of the moon from the earth.[167]

A horse may win by a nose but receives ten times the prize money of the second placegetter. Of course, the winning horse isn't ten times faster, just ever-so-slightly better on the day. However, this difference in performance is rarely due to luck or chance. Quite likely it was the cumulative impact of many micro decisions that made all the difference: the extra laps during training, the tighter discipline with the horse's nutrition or the extra diligence in planning and preparation by the jockey.[168]

Bringing this back to an everyday context, Jeff Olsen highlights how the Law of Cumulative Effect can affect our lives for good or for ill:

The things that create success in the long run don't look like they are having any impact at all in the short term...

If you don't exercise today, you won't suddenly drop dead, and you won't suddenly put on 20 pounds, and you won't suddenly lose all your muscle tone. That simple error of judgment, compounded over time, will ruin your health – but not immediately. It is the same with your health, your diet, your exercise, your financial habits, your knowledge, your relationships, your marriage, your spiritual health.[169]

We all know this of course. From the youngest age we learn that 'you are what you eat'. And yet we have an uncanny ability as humans to know something to be true but carry on as if it were not – or at least as if we will be the exception to the rule. This fascinating quirk of human psychology is known as cognitive dissonance.

The core principle of consistency is this: the impact of our choices, good or bad, may not show up for months or years, but show up it will. The chickens always come home to roost. You always reap what you sow. An inconvenient truth at times, but truth nonetheless.

So let's be real. If the level of success and momentum you are experiencing today personally or professionally is anything short of what you would like, the reason for this likely lies in things you chose to do or not do months, years and even decades ago. Momentum is the ultimate lagging indicator in life and business.

Now for the good news. You can't change what you have or haven't done in the past but you can start making choices that, compounded over time, can mean your future looks exactly as you would hope it to. Remember this Chinese proverb: the best time to plant a tree is 20 years ago; the second best time is now.

And better yet, while achieving consistency may not be easy, it is refreshingly simple.

In the remainder of this section, I want to offer five simple keys to achieving consistency that will result in massive momentum and breakthrough results in every area of your professional and personal life.

There is no substitute for doing the right things in a focused way long enough to see the results.

KEY
01

Don't wait for emotion

Motivation is often overrated. Sure, it feels good to be inspired, but sometimes we've simply got to summon up our willpower, set out in a positive direction and let our fickle emotions catch up. Nike's slogan really ought to be a motto for life: Just do it.

Waiting for inspiration to kick in before you get started is a bit like saying to a fireplace, 'You give me heat and I'll feed you some wood.' Relying on emotion to spur action is also profoundly disempowering because it puts you at the mercy of the fickle whims of emotion and sentiment. While relegating responsibility to your mood may be tempting, it puts you in the passenger seat of life.

That said, we all know what it's like to be in a funk – the lure of lethargy and the gravity of inertia. That extra hour in bed seems entirely justified. Next week seems like a good time to get started. We effortlessly become masters of procrastination and can articulate beautifully what we're going to do – tomorrow.

And yet, contrary to conventional wisdom, taking positive steps is often easier *done* than *said*. Action is the best cure for apathy.

Knowing what we should be doing and putting it off can feel like an oppressive cloud that follows us around all day. The longer we delay, the harder it can feel to get started and the less inspired we become. A vicious downward rut-cycle begins.

10 TIPS FOR GETTING OUT OF A RUT

Here are ten simple and effective ways to break the rut-cycle and get moving when you feel stuck. These are perhaps more important now than ever, with growing numbers of employees working from home, without the inbuilt accountability and structure of an office environment.

However, they can be just as helpful if you need to get yourself off the couch to mow the lawn, off the fast food to lose some weight, or off square one to write that school essay:

01

Accomplish the insignificant

Believe it or not, research has shown that doing something as insignificant as making your bed every morning is correlated with better productivity, a greater sense of wellbeing, and stronger skills at sticking with a budget. Starting your day with a small but positive activity starts a chain reaction that helps you make other good choices throughout the day.[170]

Just as discussed earlier, there is great power in taking simple steps rather than trying to leap for the stars from a standing start.

02

Get a drink of water

If you find yourself sitting at your desk, staring at the screen, unable to summon the energy or focus to do what you need to do next, try getting up and grabbing yourself a glass of water. Not only is water refreshing and enormously helpful for brain function, the physical activity and change of scenery may help you press the reset button.

03

Have a shower

While this may not always be a practical solution, showers have the unique ability to spark creativity and change our mental state.

Renowned neuroscientist Alice Flaherty argues that this is due to the fact that having a shower releases the creativity-enhancing chemical dopamine in our brains. To this point, *West Wing* writer Aaron Sorkin is famous for taking up to eight showers per day to help overcome writer's block.

04

Get physical

Exercise not only oxygenates our blood but it also releases endorphins, which can have a remarkably positive effect on our mood when we're feeling sluggish. Never forget that motion precedes emotion.[171] It doesn't need to be much – a short brisk walk around the office or even some stretches can be sufficient. The key is to not waste time trying to shift your mental state without shifting your physical state. If in doubt, get moving.

05

Show you care

Introspection is the cousin of inertia, so the best way to get out of a mental funk is to shift the focus from yourself onto someone else. Send an encouraging text message, or simply pick up the phone and tell that special someone you love them.

We are social beings and although it is tempting to isolate yourself when feeling in a rut, reaching out and making a connection is often much more helpful. Typically, you'll feel positive effects thanks to your efforts to show love and care to others. There is a reason why it is better to give than receive.

#163

10 TIPS FOR GETTING OUT OF A RUT

06

Change your environment

As we have previously discussed, this could be as simple as varying your schedule or rearranging the furniture. Other times it can involve getting out into nature in order to clear your head and look beyond present circumstances.

When I am writing, I find that I need to start my day working somewhere enjoyable and inspiring like a local café. Naturally, our environment is not just physical but relational too. If you're feeling stuck, try getting out and surrounding yourself with positive, inspired people – especially if they are already experiencing the results you're working towards.

07

Make a 'done list'

While some Type-A personalities flourish on long to-do lists, the rest of the population can find that beginning the day with a formidable task schedule is the very thing that prevents them from getting started in the first place. Try cheating a little by kicking off your day by writing a 'done' list before you turn your attention to your to-do list.[172] Not only does a list of completed tasks look impressive on paper, but it also helps build a sense of progress and achievement.

08

Remember past victories

When you feel like the weight of the world is holding you back, reflect on how you have overcome similar ruts in the past. Sometimes all you need is to recall what was effective previously so you can replicate it – after all, what works in giving you a kick start will be different from what works for others. The other benefit of remembering how you've conquered ruts in the past is that it offers a reminder that the rut you're in won't be permanent – it wasn't last time and it won't be this time. This truth alone can help give perspective and inspiration.

09

Pump up the jam

Music can be incredibly motivating – there is a good reason why gyms play tunes of a certain genre and tempo. Even in a lower-octane sense, music has a unique ability to tap into our emotions, as movie score composers know well. Try putting together a playlist of tunes that gets your blood pumping and lifts your spirits.

10

Don't beat yourself up

When you're in a funk, the worst thing you can do is feel guilty about it. Cut yourself some slack; we've all been there. Embrace the rut so that once you emerge, you might be able to lend a helping hand to the next person you come across who is in their own.

As founder of Habitat for Humanity Millard Fuller suggests: 'You don't think yourself into a new way of acting, you act yourself into a new way of thinking.' The simple message is this: while it's great to be inspired, don't make inspiration a prerequisite for getting started.

#165

Action is the best cure for apathy.

KEY
02

Count the cost

The second key to achieving consistency is to realise that being consistent isn't easy and to make peace with that reality.

Sure, the price of discipline is high – but if you choose not to pay the price of discipline, you are left with only one other choice: to pay the price of regret. That's it – two choices.

As the Bhagavad Gita says, 'We are kept from our goal not by obstacles but by a clear path to a lesser goal.'

The stoic resilience required to persist in the face of hardship, frustration or boredom is something our grandparents were more comfortable with. After all, they were raised being told that life was never meant to be easy. So when the going got tough, they perceived this as an indication they were on the right path.

In contrast, younger generations have been raised with almost the opposite message. My first body of research focused on the key drivers of youth culture. Over the space of almost four years, I interviewed over 80 000 teenagers around the world in an effort to understand the core underlying beliefs and values of modern adolescents. One trend that stood out no matter where I travelled around the globe was a core assumption among young people that life is actually meant to be easy, convenient and exciting. When the job, the relationship or the university subject gets hard or boring, young people tend to unconsciously draw the conclusion that there is something wrong with the goal they have set or that there is something wrong with them personally. Is it any wonder adolescent mental health and resilience are such pressing issues in the West?

Further still, the consistency required to build momentum rarely wins you any applause along the way. Again this is a challenge for social media addicts who live their lives with the express purpose of getting as many likes, shares and

#169

comments as possible. The reality is that private victories always precede public ones. Any time you see a person or organisation kicking goals publicly and receiving accolades, remember that their public victories are little more than the sum total of a long road of hard-fought private victories. They may have been victories of refusing to yield to apathy, ethical shortcuts, or the path of least resistance. Regardless of the form these victories took, in all likelihood they were won out of the spotlight and far from the applause of others.

Now before we get too serious here, the good news is that although consistency is often a hard, lonely and private road, it is always a road worth travelling because the destination is amazing. This is why having a clear and compelling vision is so vital – it will sustain you along the way.

Mediocrity can be jealous.

Remember too that others may not understand your dogged commitment and may even feel threatened to the point of ridiculing you. Mediocrity can be jealous like that.

CASE STUDY {

iPod: The four-year overnight success story

While Apple's breakthrough product, the iPod, was often seen as an overnight success, in hindsight the reality was very different. The iPod was by no means the first MP3 player to be released – Apple was actually quite late to the game. In 2001 when Apple released the iPod, they went from 30 per cent revenue growth the previous year to −33 per cent.

The following year, 2002, was also a negative growth year at −2 per cent. But 2003 saw a shift to a positive 18 per cent. Growth came again in 2004, up to 33 per cent. Then in 2005 momentum finally kicked in and in the blink of an eye, the iPod catapulted to 68 per cent revenue growth and gained just over a 70 per cent share of the MP3 player market.

It was Apple's very discipline and consistency throughout the early 2000s that unlocked success and created unstoppable momentum a few short years later.[173]

KEY
03

Celebrate progress

Congratulations on still reading. The previous few pages didn't pull any punches. Consistency is hard, but it doesn't have to be tiresome and soul-destroying. In fact, quite the opposite. In order to stick with any worthwhile but challenging endeavour, celebrating wins along the way is vital to maintaining motivation.

Celebration of victories builds confidence and helps give us a sense of forward progress, which means we will be less willing to turn our backs on hard-won gains. Better still, having achievable, perceivable future goals with a reward attached helps counter this drift towards the path of least resistance. Without celebration of key wins and

milestones, consistency can feel like overwhelming and endless drudgery.

One colleague of mine has developed a practice for celebrating every time his team make a sale by ringing a bell in the office. Not only does this give quantifiable and tangible value to the work his team does every day, but it also reminds everyone in the office that consistently doing the basics required to make a sale has a clear purpose and outcome. Better still, because the culture of the office is deliberately noncompetitive, one team member's sale is not de-motivating to colleagues. Rather it helps build confidence, belief and enthusiasm. The more they celebrate, the more results they get and so on.

Celebrating wins in this way becomes generative. As discussed in the opening pages of this book, success truly breeds success.

Without celebration of key wins and milestones, consistency can feel like overwhelming and endless drudgery.

If you are just starting out in business, take the time to celebrate even the smallest wins. The day your website goes live for the first time, your first paying client, your first referral. Celebrating these wins, regardless of how seemingly insignificant, powerfully convinces your unconscious mind that hard work will be worth it – after all, if the small wins count, the big wins certainly will.

> **If you are just starting out in business, take the time to celebrate even the smallest wins.**

One side benefit of celebrating progress is that it also helps clear the decks. Here's what I mean. Incomplete tasks have a unique ability to drain our mental energy.[174]

It's a bit like having 35 applications open on your computer and wondering why your CPU usage is through the roof. By celebrating completed tasks, you allow your mind to move on from them, which has the same effect as shutting down all unnecessary applications on your computer. It gives a certain sense of satisfaction, plus everything runs much faster and more smoothly afterward.

Remember, progress is a critical ingredient for perseverance. It's hard to persevere when we feel like our efforts are making no difference. Unless there is a sense of forward movement and progress, you will quickly become discouraged or despondent. In contrast, tangibly celebrating even insignificant progress can be incredibly motivating.

Progress is a critical ingredient for perseverance.

KEY
04

Pick a sustainable pace

The early stages of any worthwhile pursuit are generally marked by an excited, frenetic pace – and this is often necessary to get off go. In much the same way, space shuttles use more fuel during the first few minutes of their flight than for the rest of their entire journey.

"

Building momentum is more of a marathon than a sprint.

However, building momentum is more of a marathon than a sprint. You can start strong out of the blocks but before long it's vital to pick a sustainable pace.

As we discussed earlier, one of the most common mistakes in embarking on any worthy pursuit is to set lofty goals from a standing start. With images of fame, fortune or fabulous success, we set a bar that is too high, only to get discouraged within days or weeks.

This is a key message I share when working with salespeople. People in sales roles are notoriously erratic. Feeling inspired? Make 20 sales calls before lunch. Just been to the annual company pep rally? Set a goal to do a month's work over the coming week in the name of getting results.

The only problem with these flurries of activity is that they rarely last. As in *The Tortoise and the Hare*, speed is of limited value – sustained consistency counts for much more.

When my wife and I had a new air-conditioning system installed at our home recently, I was interested to read through the various brochures to learn just how high-tech these systems have become. In the end, we decided to go with one system over the rest largely because it had a variable fan feature called ESP, or Energy Smart Performance.

#177

The technician described the value of this feature, saying, 'Most air-conditioners have an inbuilt thermostat, which means that once the ideal temperature is reached, the compressor switches off until the temperature dips below or rises above the set mark again. This constant switching on and off of the compressor chews up a lot of power and means your unit is always in catch-up mode.'

He continued, 'Units with ESP work differently. Once the ideal temperature is reached, the unit slows down, never switching off, but maintaining the constant temperature on a low-power setting. This one feature alone cuts up to half of your electricity usage each year and puts much less strain on the compressor unit – meaning it lasts far longer.'

I was sold.

It's much the same for our cars. We all know that city driving puts an enormous strain on a car's engine due to the constant stopping and starting. In comparison, cars that mainly drive on open roads stay in fine shape mechanically for years, despite often travelling much greater distances than their urban counterparts.

Put simply, baby steps rather than binges of activity are the key to achieving sustainable momentum in business and life. You'd be far better to do three productive activities every weekday than 15 activities in rapid succession one day and then coasting for the other four.[175] Why? Because every time you stop, it requires enormous willpower and energy to get started again. In comparison, it takes far less energy to keep doing something once you've started.

Consider the hypothetical example of two planes flying from Los Angeles to New York – one flying direct, the other landing and taking off again at every state in between. Even if the second plane travelled more than twice the speed of the first in between its stops, it would take at least ten times longer and burn through much more fuel. That is the power of taking off once and then maintaining a regular sustainable pace – even if it is slower than the 'stop/ starters' around you.[176]

Remember Newton's First Law of Motion: The tendency of a body in motion is to keep moving; the tendency of a body at rest is to stay motionless. Choose a pace you can sustain and then stick with it.

Taking this one step further, I even avoid entirely switching off over weekends. Sure, I do less and try to protect time with my family while I am not at the office, but I find that if I still do one or two productive work-related things over the weekend, no matter how small or simple, it is much easier to get back up to speed come Monday morning. Sound extreme? Try it yourself next weekend and watch the difference.

CASE {
STUDY {

Water pump wisdom

In his excellent book *The Compound Effect*, Darren Hardy uses the metaphor of a hand-drawn water pump to describe the vital importance of consistency in building momentum. He explains how much dogged effort it takes: pumping the handle for quite some time, in order to create enough of a vacuum to bring the water up into the pipe. After a bit of effort and pumping, a few drops of water will come through the spout:

This is when a lot of people say 'You've got to be kidding me! All this pumping, and for what – a few measly drops? Forget it!'

Many people throw their hands up in defeat and quit, but wise people persist further. And here's where the magic happens: if you continue to pump, it doesn't take long before you'll get a full and steady stream of water. All you have to do to keep the pressure is just to pump the lever consistently. Now, what happens if you let go of the lever for too long, the water falls back down into the ground and you're back to square one. Momentum is gone.[177]

KEY
05

Aim for autopilot

The fifth and final key to achieving momentum-building consistency is to leverage the power of habit to keep you on track rather than relying on willpower.

Recent research published by Duke University found that more than 40 per cent of the actions we perform each day are not the result of any conscious decision but are rather performed by habit – on autopilot.[178]

Leadership guru Dr John C. Maxwell suggests that great power lies in our daily routine habits: 'You will never change your life until you change something you do on a daily basis', he says. 'The secret of your success is found in your daily routine.'

Habits and routines are all-pervasive little things. Aristotle knew this: 'We are what we repeatedly do', he said.

Legendary nineteenth-century philosopher and psychologist William James said much the same thing 2300 years later: 'All our life is but a mass of small habits.'

> **"**
> **Habits and routines are all-pervasive little things.**

CASE STUDY

Alcoa's bad
habits
{

How do habits play out within an organisation or business? Aluminium giant Alcoa offers a powerful example, as Charles Duhigg details in his book *The Power of Habit*.

When Paul O'Neill took the reins at Alcoa in October 1987, he seemed an unlikely choice for CEO of one of the world's largest companies. Having been a government bureaucrat for much of his career, he was a complete unknown to many in the business world.

Not only did O'Neill seem an unorthodox choice, but he also began his tenure as CEO in a similarly unorthodox way: with a focus on worker safety.

While many industry insiders and market analysts questioned the sense of this emphasis, O'Neill stuck to his guns, saying,

If you want to understand how Alcoa is doing, you need to look at our workplace safety figures. Safety will be an indicator that we're making progress in changing our habits across the entire institution.

Within a year of O'Neill's appointment, Alcoa's profits would hit a record high and by the time O'Neill retired in 2000, the company's annual net income was five times larger than before he arrived – all while Alcoa became one of the safest companies in the world.

Perhaps most ingenious of all was that, while worker safety was a worthy goal in itself, O'Neill's emphasis on it was actually part of a much broader transformation strategy leveraging the power of habit.

I knew I had to transform Alcoa. But you can't order people to change. That's not how the brain works. So I decided I was going to start by focusing on one thing. If I could start disrupting the habits around one thing, it would spread throughout the entire company.

O'Neill knew that some habits could start a chain reaction, leading to other habits being changed as they moved through an organisation.

The brilliance of O'Neill's choice to focus on safety was that no-one wanted to argue about it – unions had been demanding it for years, employees saw it as a right, and managers knew the cost due to lost productivity and morale. In a strategic masterstroke, O'Neill's plan for getting zero injuries resulted the most radical realignment in Alcoa's history. To protect workers, Alcoa needed to become far more streamlined and efficient. The new protocols that protected workers also reduced costs and increased quality and productivity. That's the power of changing habits.[179]

The dark side of habit

Naturally, habits have just as much potential to do harm as to do good. I sometimes illustrate this from the stage by having a volunteer come up from the audience. I ask them to put out their hands and I then wrap a single strand of cotton sewing thread around their wrists and ask them to try and snap the strand. Naturally, the volunteer has no trouble doing so. However, I then wrap the cotton thread around their wrists again: this time, not one thread, but rather five or ten. Even the strongest, burliest men have trouble breaking the multiple strands of cotton.

Habits work in much the same way. At first they hold very little power over us. However, over time and with repetition, they become stronger and more ingrained. As legendary investor Warren Buffett has said, 'The chains of habit are too light to be felt until they are too heavy to be broken.'

The reality is that, as sixteenth-century English poet John Drydon said, 'First we make our habits, and then our habits make us.' We are all self-made men and women, but only the successful take credit for it.[180]

Recently rewatching *The Iron Lady* starring Meryl Streep, I was struck by the insight in one particular scene where Margaret Thatcher is responding to the probing questions of a well-intentioned but, in Thatcher's view, misguided psychologist. While the scene is a work of fiction, I can almost imagine the Iron Lady herself uttering the words of wisdom Streep's character says:

Watch your thoughts because they become words.

Watch your words because they become actions.

Watch your actions because they become habits.

And watch your habits, because they determine your destiny.

So if habits are so powerful, how can we ensure they are working on our behalf, helping us consistently maintain the very focused activities we have discovered are critical for building momentum? And how can we change self-sabotaging habits that are getting in the way of that goal?

Baby steps rather than binges of activity are the key to achieving sustainable momentum.

CASE
STUDY

Getting an
exercise habit

In order for an organisation or individual to achieve consistency over time, willpower and good intentions are not enough. The power of habit is that constructive actions become an automatic response.

I discovered this a few years ago when I reached the age of 30 and realised it was time to take health and fitness more seriously. I had been a rep swimmer in my teens, so the discipline of exercise was not unfamiliar to me. Throughout my twenties I had tried nearly everything in an effort to recapture the fitness motivation I had enjoyed in my younger days. But nothing seemed to stick. Momentum just never kicked in.

A turning point for me was speaking with a colleague who is a peak performance and fitness coach. 'After the age of 30,' he told me, 'an inactive person will lose about 1 per cent of their muscle mass each year.'

What a terrifying thought. I was convinced – now was the time to get fit and stay toned. But I knew that I had to find a way to make this commitment more enduring than previous well-intentioned resolutions.

The solution struck me one day and it was so simple I almost dismissed it.

'What if I just go to the gym every second day? That way, I'll know that if I haven't gone the day before, today's my day.'

So I thought I'd give it a try and, to my astonishment, it worked! Because the established routine was simple and systematic, it was one I could keep even when my schedule was at its busiest. What's more, it took the element of decision out of going to the gym. In the past, any excuse for deferring exercise seemed reasonable. If I had a long day, felt a bit fatigued, or was travelling and staying in hotels, the gym could always wait till tomorrow. And very often tomorrow never came. But my new routine, while somewhat flexible, forced me to find ways around these excuses.

For the first time in my life I began travelling with exercise clothes in my suitcase and only booked to stay at hotels with a gym.

Three years down the track, I am pleased to report that my systematic approach to fitness is still working. In fact, I realised just how ingrained and enjoyable my routine had become when I was visiting family recently and discovered that I had forgotten to pack my gym clothes. I was genuinely disappointed to not be able to work out – and genuinely surprised by my reaction. After all, three years previous I would have relished the mistake and seen it as a very worthy excuse for a few days off.

And that's the power of developing systematic routines and sticking with them till they become habitual. Again, Dr John C. Maxwell's words ring true: 'You will never change your life until you change something you do daily. The secret of your success is found in your daily routine.'

Changing habits

First things first — is it really possible to change an ingrained habit? The good news is that the answer to this question is a resounding yes. Researchers at University College London set out in 2009 to ask this question. They were looking for the moment when an altered behaviour becomes automatic or ingrained. Having ascertained that sustained habit change was indeed possible, they then tested how long such a change might take. The point of 'automaticity', as they called it, came on average after 66 days — a number that is at odds with the unfounded 21-day figure thrown around in the world of pop psychology.[181]

So if we know habit change is possible and how long it takes to occur, what is the process involved?

It's valuable to remember that even small and insignificant habit shifts can lead to disproportionately significant change.

Charles Duhigg in his book *The Power of Habit* offers some helpful insights. He points to the fact that habits are actually a three-step loop: the cue, the routine and finally the reward. (This final step reinforces the importance of celebrating progress, as discussed earlier.)

According to Duhigg's research, the way to change a habit is to focus on changing the middle element (the routine) because it is easier to convince someone to adopt a new behaviour if there is something familiar at the beginning and the end. Therefore, to change a habit, use the same cue, provide the same reward, but shift the routine. Consider how smokers usually can't quit unless they find some activity to replace cigarettes when their nicotine craving is triggered. This research finding has powerfully influenced treatments for alcoholism, obesity, obsessive-compulsive disorders and hundreds of other destructive behaviours.[182]

Interestingly, recent research underscores the importance of altering routines early on in the habit-change process. In the case of quitting smoking, the first week can make all the difference. Studies have found that people who don't smoke in the first week after they have decided to quit are nine times more likely to follow through and be able to actually stop smoking permanently. The lesson here is that, while habit change can take up to 66 days on average, never underestimate the power of getting momentum early in the process.

At a personal level, habits become most powerful when they are linked to an individual's identity. Once someone has incorporated a new habit into their identity, something powerful occurs. Consider the shift that occurs when someone sees themself as an athlete getting stronger every day, rather than as a couch potato trying to change their ways.

Stepping back from the world of behavioural psychology, what does this insight mean for you and me as we look to form constructive and momentum-building habits?

Well, firstly, it's valuable to remember that even small and insignificant habit shifts can lead to disproportionately significant change.

Australian researchers Megan Oaten and Ken Cheng suggest that the simplest approach is to focus on forming one positive habit and allowing this change to affect others.

Oaten and Cheng have found evidence in their studies that students who successfully acquired one positive habit reported less stress; less impulsive spending; better dietary habits; decreased alcohol, tobacco and caffeine consumption; and fewer hours watching TV. As we discussed in previous pages, this positive habit could be as simple as starting your day by making your bed. It would appear that changing one habit not only makes the changed habit easier to stick with, but also makes it easier to change other habits as well.[183]

Sound too good to be true?

In a similar study, James Prochaska at the University of Rhode Island looked at the power of adding the habit of exercise into a person's daily routine – and the findings were equally compelling. When people start exercising habitually, even as infrequently as once per week, they start changing other unrelated patterns in their lives, often unconsciously. For example, people who exercised started eating better and became more productive at work. They smoked less, showed greater patience with colleagues and family, used credit cards less frequently and reported feeling less stressed. 'There's something about [exercise] that makes other good habits easier', explained Prochaska.[184]

Whether at an individual or organisational level, never underestimate the power of simple, daily and insignificant habits. They can often act like the small rudder that steers an enormous ship.

This third and final element of the momentum equation may not be the sexiest or most enjoyable, but consistency really is the secret sauce to building unstoppable momentum in business and life. Sure, it may be hard and there are days when the cost seems high. But remember, if lasting success were easy, everyone would have it.

DEFYING GRAVITY

If you have never experienced the thrill of unpowered flight, it is definitely something to put on your bucket list.

One of the best gifts I received for my thirtieth birthday was a gift voucher for a glider flight – something I had always wanted to do.

For those who are unaware, the process of gliding involves being towed up to 1500 feet by a powered aircraft – and then being released.

I arrived at the aerodrome early in the morning on the scheduled day of my glider flight and I remember being both nervous and excited.

> **The moment I squeezed into the back seat of the glider, I knew this was the point of no return.**

The moment I squeezed into the back seat of the glider, I knew this was the point of no return. As my pilot Gary and I climbed higher and higher, being towed by a single-engine Cessna, I was struck by the fact that the ride was bumpier than any flight I had been on. The glider felt incredibly volatile, even under power.

Just as I was wondering if this gift really was such a great idea after all, there was a loud clicking sound followed by silence. The tow-rope had been released and we were gliding.

As I watched our tow plane bank off to the left, the thought suddenly dawned on me – Gary and I were airborne, with no engine and no plan B. The sensation was like nothing I'd ever experienced before. Apart from the gushing of wind as it passed the air vent near my right ear, there was no sound or vibration at all. It was exhilarating.

The gliding school's brochure talked about what they called a controlled descent – something I assumed we would start on pretty much straight away. But ten minutes later, we didn't appear to be descending. In fact, a quick glance over Gary's shoulder at the altimeter showed that we were actually 800 feet higher than we had been at the release point.

By the 45-minute mark, we were still flying high and I became intrigued.

I asked Gary how long gliders can stay airborne for and he informed me that just the year before, a world record had been set in New Zealand – 15 hours of unpowered flight. Almost the time it takes to fly from Sydney to Los Angeles.

Gary could tell I was intrigued by this revelation and so he went on to explain how gliding works.

The key to staying airborne is to ride thermal air currents or updrafts. But you've got to stay alert and know what you're looking for. As one thermal dissipates, you've got to be ready to join the next one. If the conditions are right, you go from one thermal current to the next – spiralling higher and higher for hours.

Reflecting on what I learned gliding at 3000 feet in the years since, I believe that precisely the same principle applies to individuals and organisations. In one sense it doesn't matter how successful you are or how high you've risen, you will inevitably lose speed and altitude unless you take deliberate steps to counteract the forces of gravity and entropy.

In the same way harnessing updrafts offers the secret to maintaining altitude for a glider, my hope is that our time together has given you the tools necessary to soar ever higher and further – maintaining momentum and vitality far longer than would otherwise be possible.

Unlike the fickle and unpredictable updrafts of thermal currents, however, the keys to riding high and mastering the art of momentum are predictable, measurable and simple. As we said at the start, there is no silver bullet or shortcut, but there is a surefire formula that works.

The question is, what will you do with it? That is a decision that is entirely yours to make. Choose well and even the sky won't be your limit.

I wish you all the very best.

Notes

1. Foster, R 2015, 'Picking the next disruption', *Business Spectator*, 27 July.

2. Hardy, D 2010, *The Compound Effect*, Vanguard Press, New York, p. 94.

3. Chaykowski, K 2015, 'Add this to Twitter's growth woes: a flock of younger social apps threatens to eclipse it', *Forbes*, 15 June.

4. Goel, V 2014, 'Twitter has a problem with your mother', *The Sydney Morning Herald*, 6 February.

5. Koh, Y 2016, 'Twitter woes mount as user growth stalls', *The Wall Street Journal*, 10 February.

6. Russolillo, S 2016, 'Why Twitter should eyeball Yahoo's past', *The Wall Street Journal*, 9 February.

7. Chaykowski, K 2015, 'Add this to Twitter's growth woes: a flock of younger social apps threatens to eclipse it', *Forbes*, 15 June.

8. Koh, Y 2015, 'Twitter names co-founder Jack Dorsey as CEO', *The Wall Street Journal*, 5 October.

9. Koh, Y 2015, 'Twitter to cut up to 8 per cent of workforce', *The Wall Street Journal*, 13 October.

10. Rigby, R 2011, *28 Business Thinkers Who Changed the World*, Kogan Page Limited, London, p. 149.

11. Tett, G 2015, *The Silo Effect*, Simon & Schuster, New York, pp. 52–4.

12. Ibid., pp. 54, 55.

13. Ibid., p. 66.

14. Ibid., pp. 77, 78.

15. Ibid.

16. Osati, S 2011, 'Steve Jobs wanted Apple to be like Sony', www.sonyrumors.net, 11 October.

17. Wakabayashi, D 2012, 'Japan's dimwitted smartphones', *The Wall Street Journal*, 16 August.

18. Kriegel, R 1991, *If it ain't broke … break it!*, Time Warner, New York, p. 74.

19. Spector, M & Mattioli, D 2012, 'Kodak teeters on the brink', *The Wall Street Journal*, 20 January.

20. Neate, R 2012, 'Kodak files for bankruptcy protection', *The Sydney Morning Herald*, 7 November.

21. Carroll, P & Mui, C 2008, *Billion Dollar Lessons*, Penguin, New York, p. 88.

22. Ibid., pp. 92–3.

23. Ibid., p. 93.

24. Ibid., p. 94.

25. Neate, R 2012, 'Kodak files for bankruptcy protection', *The Sydney Morning Herald*, 7 November.

26. Carroll, P & Mui, C 2008, *Billion Dollar Lessons*, Penguin, New York, p. 88.

27. Ibid., p. 98.

28. Neate, R 2012, 'Kodak files for bankruptcy protection', *The Sydney Morning Herald*, 7 November.

29. Mackay, H 2011, 'Where there's faith, so too doubt', *The Sydney Morning Herald*, 26 December.

30. Proverbs 16:18, *The Holy Bible – New Living Translation*, Tyndale House, Wheaton IL, 1996.

31. Christensen, C 2000, *The Innovator's Dilemma*, HarperBusiness, New York, p. xiv.

32. Larreche, J 2008, *The Momentum Effect*, Wharton School Publishing, New Jersey, p. 51.

33. Landes, D 2000, *Revolution in Time*, Harvard University Press, Cambridge.

34. Thompson, J 2009, '1969: Seiko's breakout year', *Watchtime*, 20 December.

35. Ibid.

36. Drucker, P 1985, *Innovation and Entrepreneurship*, HarperCollins, New York, p. 126.

37. Collins, J & Porras, J 1994, *Built to Last*, HarperCollins, New York, p. 81.

38. Duhigg, C 2014, *The Power of Habit*, Random House, New York, pp. 160–4.

39. Linkner, J 2014, *The Road to Reinvention*, Jossey-Bass, San Francisco, p. 77.

40. Birchall, A 2012, 'The brains behind bureaucracy', *Management Today*, May.

41. Kriegel, R 1991, *If it ain't broke…break it!*, Time Warner, New York, p. 117.

42. Obama, B 2012, 'State of the Union Address Transcript', *Washington Post*, 24 January.

43. Larreche, J 2008, *The Momentum Effect*, Wharton School Publishing, New Jersey, p. 222.

44. Troianovski, A & Grundenberg, S 2012, 'Nokia's bad call on smartphones', *The Wall Street Journal*, 18 July.

45. 2011, IBS Case Development Centre, 'Case studies on innovation', p. 21.

46. Carroll, P & Mui, C 2008, *Billion Dollar Lessons*, Penguin, New York, p. 226.

47. Linkner, J 2014, *The Road to Reinvention*, Jossey-Bass, San Francisco, p. 28.

48. Eichenwald, K 2012, 'Microsoft's lost decade', *Vanity Fair*, August.

49. Linkner, J 2014, *The Road to Reinvention*, Jossey-Bass, San Francisco, p. 58.

50. Nocera, J 2012, 'Has Apple peaked?', *The New York Times*, 24 September.

51. Ovide, S 2013, 'Next CEOs biggest job: Fixing Microsoft's culture', *The Wall Street Journal*, 25 August.

52. Eichenwald, K 2012, 'Microsoft's lost decade', *Vanity Fair*, August.

53. Ibid.

54. Ibid.

55. Ibid.

56. Ibid.

57. Ibid.

58. Ibid.

59. Ovide, S 2014, 'Microsoft bucks trend as sales defy expectations', *The Wall Street Journal*, 23 October.

60. Proverbs 29:18, *The Holy Bible – New Living Translation*, Tyndale House, Wheaton IL, 1996.

61. Munsey, P. 2008, *Legacy Now*, Charisma House, Florida, pp. 159-60.

62. Kouzes, J & Posner, B 2006, *A Leader's Legacy*, Jossey-Bass, San Francisco, pp. 99-102.

63. Kriegel, R 1991, *If it ain't broke… break it!*, Time Warner, New York, p. 33.

64. Collins, J. 2004, *Good to Great*, Random House, London, pp. 165-66.

65. Hardy, D 2010, *The Compound Effect*, Vanguard Press, New York, p. 69.

66. Linkner, J 2014, *The Road to Reinvention*, Jossey-Bass, San Francisco, pp. 7-9.

67. Heath, C & Heath, D 2010, *Switch*, Broadway Books, New York, pp. 67-71.

68. 2011, IBS Case Development Centre, 'Case studies on innovation' p. 20.

69. Ibid., p. 134.

70. Calonia, J 2014, '5 Secrets to Mastering Dave Ramsey's Debt Snowball Method', *The Huffington Post*, I October.

71. Hagger, M 2010, 'Ego depletion and strength model of self-control', *Psychology Bulletin*, July.

72. Krupp, S 2015, '6 strategies great leaders use for long-term success', *Business Insider*, 19 May.

73. Linkner, J 2014, *The Road to Reinvention*, Jossey-Bass, San Francisco, p. 34.

74. Mitchell, S 2015, 'Coca-Cola, Pepsi under pressure as millennials ditch sugar', *The Sydney Morning Herald*, 23 July.

75. Esterl, M 2014, 'Share a Coke credited with pop in sales', *The Wall Street Journal*, 25 September.

76. Knight, E 2015, 'Has Coca-Cola lost its cool?', *The Sydney Morning Herald*, 18 February.

77. Jervell, E 2015, 'How Adidas aims to get its cool back', *The Wall Street Journal*, 22 March.

78. Germano, S 2015, 'Nike's challenge: staying ahead of the pack', *The Wall Street Journal*, 20 September.

79. Jervell, E 2015, 'Adidas puts some spring in its step', *The Wall Street Journal*, 20 August.

80. Jervell, E 2015, 'Adidas profit rises on robust US sales, rebound at Reebok', *The Wall Street Journal*, 5 May.

81. Kriegel, R 1991, *If it ain't broke…break it!*, Time Warner, New York, p. 76.

82. Kriegel, R & Brandt, D 1997, *Sacred Cows Make the Best Burgers*, Time Warner, New York, pp. 54, 55.

83. Kriegel, R 1991, *If it ain't broke…break it!*, Time Warner, New York, pp. 2, 69.

84. Jargon, J 2015, 'Sbarro seeks new life outside the mall', *The Wall Street Journal*, 2 October.

85. Collins, J & Porras, J 1994, *Built to Last*, HarperCollins, New York, p. 8.

86. Ibid., p. 47.

87. Collins, J 2009, *How the Mighty Fall*, Random House Business Books, London, p. 53.

88. This is an excerpt from a presentation delivered by Howard Schultz on 21 April 2011 as part of a publicity tour for his book *Onward*.

89. Ibid.

90. Duhigg, C 2014, *The Power of Habit*, Random House, New York, pp. 149–52.

91. Carroll, P & Mui, C 2008, *Billion Dollar Lessons*, Penguin, New York, p. 117.

92. Cohan, P 2011, 'How success killed Eastman Kodak', *Forbes*, 1 October.

93. Carroll, P & Mui, C 2008, *Billion Dollar Lessons*, Penguin, New York, p. 138.

94. Koziol, M 2015, '10 product flops that outdo Coke life', *The Sydney Morning Herald*, 26 May.

95. England, L 2015, 'Here's what's inside the little red book that is placed on the desk of every Facebook employee', *Business Insider*, 29 May.

96. McSpadden, K 2015, 'You now have a shorter attention span than a goldfish', *Time*, 14 May.

97. Kim, L 2016, 'Multitasking is killing your brain', *Medium*, 15 February.

98. Silverman, R 2012, 'Workplace distractions: here's why you won't finish this article', *The Wall Street Journal*, 11 December.

99. Anderson, C 2016, 'Finally, evidence that taking a nap at work is good for business', *The Huffington Post*, 11 February.

100. Keller, G 2013, *The One Thing*, John Murray Publishers, London, p. 51.

101. Zack, D 2015, *Singletasking*, Berrett-Koehler Publishers, Oakland, p. 7.

102. Weinschenk, S 2012, 'The true cost of multi-tasking', *Psychology Today*, 18 September.

103. Silverman, R 2012, 'Workplace distractions: here's why you won't finish this article', *The Wall Street Journal*, 11 December.

104. Kim, L 2016, 'Multitasking is killing your brain', *Medium*, 15 February.

105. Ibid.

106. Ibid.

107. Ibid.

108. Silverman, R 2012, 'Workplace distractions: here's why you won't finish this article', *The Wall Street Journal*, 11 December.

109. Berry, S 2016, 'Attention residue: why focusing on multiple tasks can kill your work performance', *The Sydney Morning Herald*, 27 January.

110. Silverman, R 2012, 'Workplace distractions: here's why you won't finish this article', *The Wall Street Journal*, 11 December.

111. Cowley, M 2012, 'Seebohm curses social media fixation after falling for own hype', *WA Today*, 31 July.

112. Orr, A 2012, 'Tweeting could cost you medals', *WA Today*, 2 August.

113. Sygall, D 2015, 'Rio Olympics 2016: Olympians grapple with social media policy, after warnings from Anna Meares, Sally Pearson and Emily Seebohm', *The Sydney Morning Herald*, 16 December.

114. Berry, S 2016, 'Attention residue: why focusing on multiple tasks can kill your work performance', *The Sydney Morning Herald*, 27 January.

115. Boardman, S 2016, 'How pressing pause improves performance', *Psychology Today*, 21 January.

116. Knight, E 2013, 'Billabong perilously close to wipeout', *The Sydney Morning Herald*, 8 April.

117. Ibid.

118. Knight, E 2013, 'Billabong advisers skim off $23m fees', *The Sydney Morning Herald*, 27 August.

119. Greenblat, E 2013, 'Billabong brand worthless as loss blows out', *The Sydney Morning Herald*, 27 August.

120. Chanthadavong, A 2013, 'Billabong to make a turnaround with simplified strategy plan', *RetailBiz*, 11 December.

121. Collins, J 2009, *How the Mighty Fall*, Random House Business Books, London, p. 55.

122. Keller, G 2013, *The One Thing*, John Murray Publishers, London, p. 192.

123. Gallo, C 2011, 'Steve Jobs: get rid of all the crappy stuff', *Forbes*, 16 May.

124. Rosenthall, J 2012, 'Steve Jobs' advice to Larry Page', *Digg*, 22 October.

125. LeClaire, J 2011, 'Larry Page-run Google shutters 7 more projects', *NewsFactor*, 23 November.

126. Keller, G 2013, *The One Thing*, John Murray Publishers, London, p. 34.

127. Wakabayashi, D 2012, 'Hitachi president prods turnaround', *The Wall Street Journal*, 10 May.

128. Wakabayashi, D 2013, 'Panasonic to pare unprofitable units', *The Wall Street Journal*, 28 March.

129. Muller, J 2004, *Plant Pruning A to Z*, Lothian, Melbourne, pp. 10, 11.

130. Ibid., p. 10.

131. Lombardi, M 1997, *Pruning Made Easy*, Ward Lock, London, p. 6.

132. Stowar, J 1998, *The Garden Adviser*, Bookman Press, Melbourne, pp. 451-2.

133. Robertson, D 2014, *Brick by Brick*, Random House, New York, p. 43.

134. Ibid., p. 98.

135. Ibid., p. 70.

136. Min-Jung, K 2012, 'Feature of the Months: Lego', *Beyond Magazine*, August.

137. Robertson, D 2013, *Brick by Brick*, Crown Business, New York, p. 3.

138. Ibid., p. 259.

139. Wilcox, K 2012, 'The block's answer to Barbie is a hit for Lego', *The Sydney Morning Herald*, 14 September.

140. Robertson, D 2014, *Brick by Brick*, Random House, New York, p. 37.

141. Ibid., pp. 62, 63.

142. Ibid., pp. 65, 66, 98.

143. Ibid., p. 130.

144. Ibid., p. 108.

145. Ibid., p. 114.

146. Ibid., p. 283.

147. Ibid., p. 216.

148. Min-Jung, K 2012, 'Feature of the Months: Lego', *Beyond Magazine*, August.

149. http://www.boeing.com/commercial/aeromagazine/aero_05/textonly/fo01txt.html, accessed 16 March 2016.

150. Wakabayashi, D 2012, 'New Sony chief executive reveals fast-forward plans', *The Wall Street Journal*, 2 February.

151. Osati, S 2011, 'Steve Jobs wanted Apple to be like Sony', *www.sonyrumors.net*, 11 October.

152. Ibid.

153. Wakabayashi, D & Takahashi, Y 2012, 'Sony's new CEO vows to "revive" company', *The Wall Street Journal*, 12 April.

154. Wakabayashi, D 2012, 'Live blog: Sony CEO Kazuo Hirai', *The Wall Street Journal*, 12 April.

155. Wakabayashi, D & Takahashi, Y 2012, 'New Sony CEO to cut 10,000 jobs', *The Wall Street Journal*, 9 April.

156. Ibid.

157. Karp, H 2015, 'Sony moves toward sale of music-publishing unit', *The Wall Street Journal*, 7 October.

158. Wakabayashi, D & Takahashi, Y 2012, 'Sony's new CEO vows to "revive" company', *The Wall Street Journal*, 12 April.

159. Ng, S 2014, 'P&G to shed more than half its brands', *The Wall Street Journal*, 1 August.

160. Worthen, B & Sherr, I 2012, 'CEO Whitman tells HPs workers "everything is on table" in overhaul', *The Wall Street Journal*, 21 March.

161. Ovide, S 2014, 'Hewlett-Packard: will slimmer make stronger?', *The Wall Street Journal*, 6 October.

162. Collins, J 2009, *How the Mighty Fall*, Random House Business Books, London, pp. 163–6.

163. Kehoe, J 2014, 'IBM struggles in new world', *The Australian Financial Review*, 22 October.

164. Ante, S 2013, 'IBM's chief to employees: think fast, move faster', *The Wall Street Journal*, 24 April.

165. Olsen, J 2013, *The Slight Edge*, Greenleaf Book Group, Austin, Texas, pp. 30–5.

166. Gladwell, M 2000, *The Tipping Point*, Abacus, London, p. 11.

167. Keller, G 2013, *The One Thing*, John Murray Publishers, London, p. 13.

168. Hardy, D 2010, *The Compound Effect*, Vanguard Press, New York, pp. 43, 44.

169. Olsen, J 2013, *The Slight Edge*, Greenleaf Book Group, Austin, Texas, pp. 55–7.

170. Duhigg, C 2014, *The Power of Habit*, Random House, New York, pp. 108–9.

171. Robertson, D 2014, *Brick by Brick*, Random House, New York, p. 118.

172. Olsen, J 2013, *The Slight Edge*, Greenleaf Book Group, Austin, Texas, p. 211.

173. Hardy, D 2010, *The Compound Effect*, Vanguard Press, New York, pp. 97, 98.

174. Olsen, J 2013, *The Slight Edge*, Greenleaf Book Group, Austin, Texas, p. 209.

175. Ibid., p. 207.

176. Hardy, D 2010, *The Compound Effect*, Vanguard Press, New York, pp. 112, 113.

177. Ibid., pp. 113–15.

178. Duhigg, C 2014, *The Power of Habit*, Random House, New York, p. xvi.

179. Ibid., pp. 97–108.

180. Hardy, D 2010, *The Compound Effect*, Vanguard Press, New York, p. 28.

181. Keller, G 2013, *The One Thing*, John Murray Publishers, London, p. 59.

182. Duhigg, C 2014, *The Power of Habit*, Random House, New York, p. 62.

183. Keller, G 2013, *The One Thing*, John Murray Publishers, London, p. 59.

184. Duhigg, C 2014, *The Power of Habit*, Random House, New York, pp. 108, 109.

Index

Keen to take your learning to the next level?

Michael's 60-day Supercharge is a unique online masterclass featuring a range of modules designed to help you implement the principles and strategies in this book.

Over the course of 60 days, you will:

· Identify the hidden factors that may be holding you back or sapping your momentum
· Develop a clear and actionable game plan for growth
· Discover a blueprint for leveraging your daily efforts for maximum impact
· Formulate a plan for managing the distractions that are currently diluting your effectiveness
· Learn how to get out of any rut and make powerful new habits that stick

To thank you for having purchased this book, we'd like to offer you a discount on course registration. Simply enter the code 'Reader' at www.60daysupercharge.com to get started supercharging your momentum today.

Connect
with WILEY ▶▶▶

WILEY

Browse and purchase the full range of Wiley publications on our official website.

www.wiley.com

Check out the Wiley blog for news, articles and information from Wiley and our authors.

www.wileybizaus.com

Join the conversation on Twitter and keep up to date on the latest news and events in business.

@WileyBizAus

Sign up for Wiley newsletters to learn about our latest publications, upcoming events and conferences, and discounts available to our customers.

www.wiley.com/email

Wiley titles are also produced in e-book formats. Available from all good retailers.

WILEY

Learn more with practical advice from our experts

Future Brain
Dr Jenny Brockis

Ignite
Gabrielle Dolan

From Me to We
Janine Garner

Selfish, Scared and Stupid
Dan Gregory and Kieran Flanagan

The Innovation Formula
Dr Amantha Imber

Innovation is a State of Mind
James O'Loghlin

The Innovation Race
Andrew and Gaia Grant

Lead with Wisdom
Mark Strom

Power Play
Yamini Naidu

Available in print and e-book formats

WILEY